CHOSEN VESSEL

A TRUE STORY

BY SUSAN WARD

CHOSEN VESSEL
by Susan Ward

Printed in the United States of America.

ISBN 9781498427326

www.xulonpress.com

DEDICATIONS

T his book is dedicated first to Jesus, without whom
I would not be here. Thank You for sharing in my
sorrow. I am grateful for Your sacrifice and for Your death
that led to life. You alone earned the right to sit with me
in darkness, yet did not deliver me from it, but rather protected me in it and brought me through it. You could have
prevented the darkness from occurring in my life, yet You
chose Your way of wisdom when you put in place the
supernatural laws in the universe in which we live. You
wrote the laws and subject yourself to them, but they are
not over You. Your wisdom is higher. You use them to
highlight and shine forth Your glory into this fallen world
and lead us to You.

To my husband, daughter, and many friends who have
stayed on this journey with me even when you couldn't
understand what I was going through. Thank you for your

love and support, and the freedom that you gave me so that I could find myself.

My counselor, Jeanne Anne Dixon, thank you for believing me, and believing in me. May you rest in the Father's arms.

ACKNOWLEDGMENTS

I've been privileged to have the help of many people during the process of writing this book.

Thank you to Cassidy Willet, and Penny Hiller for your advice, editing expertise, and friendship. You took on a project that would stretch your mind and spirit, and for that I am grateful.

To Dana, Vickie, Deb, Pam, Jen, and Karen, and many others who helped with advice, council, proofreading, and just listening to me when I was desperate for fresh insight. Your friendship has meant more than you'll ever know, this side of heaven.

Thank you all.

TABLE OF CONTENTS

PREFACE

Evil is a reality that we are forced to live with in this world. Being exposed to evil that is beyond our mind's comprehension will not corrupt our souls. For we are not to focus on evil, or study it, or deny it, but we are to expose it. It is only by being exposed that evil can be overcome by good.

This book is about my life: how God took me from the hands of darkness and brought me into His light.

One Saturday afternoon in January 1993, I was sitting on my couch reading the mail. I heard the voice of God so clearly that I looked up half expecting to see Him standing right in front of me.

He said, "I want you to tell My church about your life."

Shocked, I blurted out, "You want me to do what?"

But in my heart, I thought, don't they already know about the devil?

Ignoring my statement of surprise, He decided to address the question that lay in my heart and simply stated, "No, they don't."

As these words were spoken, images began to blossom in my mind. I saw many faces and crowds of thousands of people from all over the world. I believe He was showing me the faces of the people who need to hear the message of this story: God's glory is revealed in the midst of darkness.

In the spring of 2004 I had a dream in which I saw the name and cover for a book that I believed God wanted me to write. This took me by surprise since I have never considered myself a writer nor have I ever had any ambition to write a book. Nevertheless, I woke up the next day knowing that I had to write about my life.

God's purposes for wanting my story told is vast and beyond my scope of knowledge. However, during the years spent writing, God has used the process to uncover and reveal the truth of who I really am and where I've come from. As a result, there has been much healing in my heart, mind, soul, and spirit.

Another reason for this book, other than my own healing: possibly the healing of many others who read or hear about it. I was unaware that God was going to use this process for that purpose, and had I known how hard it was going to be, I may not have done it.

Although God has brought clarity and healing during the process of writing this book, He has also further exposed the reality about the evil that is at work in this world. Much of this story, and the evil that is described is beyond what most people can grasp, understand, or believe. That we live in such a world as I describe in these pages does not bring much comfort, but that God lives in it with us, bringing light into the darkness, proves that He really is the Comfort of the world.

The revelations and memories are told in a somewhat chaotic fashion. I did this for one reason: I wanted you, the reader, to have a glimpse into the madness of what it is like to wake up one day to a life that is unrecognizable, to realize that all you ever thought was true, was in fact not. My life at age 29, as I had known and thought it to be, was nothing more than a facade that hid countless horrors behind the protective walls in mind. Yet after all those years of seemingly protecting me, the walls began crumbling.

So as I set off and began to unravel the mystery of my past, I discovered that my mind had stored many of my memories from childhood in layers. I believe this was a survival mechanism to ensure that I would not break when the reality of what happened began to the surface. The earliest and most severe memories were broken and robotic, seemingly without emotion, because of my mind's inability to process the horrific abuse that was taking place. The information from the most severe abuses had been separated into different memory files. Some files contained the physical pain of the memory, others held the emotions, still others held one of the five senses (touch, sight, audio, smell, or taste) associated with the experience. For example, there were times I would see what was happening but could not hear or feel what was being done. There were other times when I could hear and feel the abuse but couldn't clearly see what was happening until later. My mind was devastated by the unimaginable horror, but it survived by breaking the memories down into manageable parts, and tiny pieces.

All the parts of any one memory did not come out at the same time as other parts. They were all painfully pieced together over a 25-year period. I take you through the layers as they were uncovered, layer by layer, part by part, each one delving deeper into the truth. I have done this purposely to convey what the trauma was really like. My life was not neat and orderly before this journey began, and it was not neat and orderly when the past came crashing through.

I was not aware of what happened during my childhood because the people who did these terrible things covered up what they were doing by using mental and physical stimulation, simulation, manipulation, and cruelty. They created memories of a normal life using visual pictures, sensory and emotional excitement, and pain — all the necessary ingredients.

They continued, day and night, to build a sequence of life events and time. The reality of where I really was during those months away from my family in the underground facilities, the abuse and the shock of what I was exposed to, were not retainable options for my brain to hold onto. Therefore, I was eager to accept the lies they were feeding me. Eventually I accepted those "memories" as my own. My life, yet not my life. I never lived it, but it became my life — my memories — events I would recite as my own, for decades to come.

Scenes from movies they showed and techniques they used caused me to lose the ability to discern what was real and what was not. I became pliable to whatever they wanted me to do. They stole my identity.

As I recovered these memories, I had to go through layers of misinformation and disinformation. At times I found myself feeling like I was speaking a completely different language from those around me. I would try to explain things that happened, but would use code names disguised as famous people or places. For years those code names caused a lot of confusion. *Did I really know these famous people? Had I seen a murder of a historical person? Was I a witness to something that the world needed to know about?* Even as those thoughts raced through my mind, I realized that I sounded like a paranoid psychopath.

It took me a long time to realize that the use of code names and any revelations about these crimes had been intended to sound unbelievable. If I ever did try to explain what had happened, I would sound like a crazed person who should be locked up and hauled off to an institution where their secrets could be kept, safely locked up in an asylum. The skill in their deception was brilliant.

I speak of my abusers as the "they" people. I call them "they" because in my mind that is who they are. There are different names, descriptions, places, and organizations that come to my mind identifying who "they" are. This information may, or may not be accurate due to the use of disinformation and misinformation they used to protect their identities and the secrecy of the experiments they carried out. Code names, programming, brainwashing, force, depravation of all things human, (food, light, touch, clothing) and other unspeakable abuses were used not only to carry out their evil, but also to cover it. Therefore, I do not know who "they" are for certain and I choose not to speculate on it here.

As I tell my story, there will be times that information seems to be missing. That is because there is. I have chosen not to fill in these gaps with plausible explanations or stories to answer questions that may arise. This is not a story book. Reality does not have all the answers.

These memories were not recalled during counseling sessions or with the use of hypnosis. The reality of what happened to me as a child came creeping in piece by piece as I tried to establish and maintain a normal adult life.

In the late 1980's, when my memories began coming closer to the surface, I had just married a wonderful man named Mimms. In the years that followed, Mimms stood by me during the chaos and craziness that ensued once the memories came forth and the programming (walls) crumbled. He was a silent but solid rock, never wavering in his commitment to me even when I was at my worst. He lived between acceptance and denial of the circumstances that overtook our lives. But he remained by my side to support me in whatever came our way. My daughter Dana, was divinely protected by God, often off with friends or other family members while I was in the midst of reliving memories and the uncontrollable behavior that came with them. Dana was vaguely aware that things were different during that time and that "Mom had some problems."

God was watchful over the process and path that my life was about to take. He had chosen a specific time to reveal Himself to me and lead me into His Kingdom, out of the kingdom of darkness and into the Kingdom of Light. But, before I would come into His Kingdom, a battle would be fought between the past and the present, good and evil, the natural and supernatural. He prepared me as best as anyone could for what was coming. He had given me a wonderful husband and daughter to hang onto me and keep me tethered to the earthly realm by their presence and support.

It was with their help, and the abundant grace of God, that I was able to come out of the darkness and into the light.

CHAPTER ONE

I always live my life as if I am in a hurry, running from one moment to the next. I'm not sure why I'm in a hurry. I just always live each new day as if I'm trying to get through it as quickly and fully as I can before death finally catches me. I don't think about dying, not consciously anyway; it's more like a subconscious belief that I won't survive to old age.

The memories I can recall of my childhood are limited. I've always thought this was a little strange, but I've never been sure what was normal for a person to remember. If I am asked about my childhood, I always respond with minimal facts. Over the years I've begun to realize I answer all questions about my childhood with the same facts, as if I'm reciting information, not remembering it. There is never any emotion or connection to what I'm saying. It's like reading lines from a play I once memorized, except the play is the story of my life rather than some fictional character.

Surely there have to be some other memories — playing, just being a kid, something. I sit down and probe my mind with any question I can think of to jog a memory. When I ask myself where I live, I recite a list of towns where I have lived and give my age at the time I lived there. When I ask myself what my favorite toy was as a child, I answer with the same lines: where I lived and age at the time. I've discovered I'm unable to remember any toys or favorite things. Whenever I try to figure out my favorite game or recall a special memory, I simply repeat the facts about my age and where I lived. Curious, I begin to wonder if everyone's memories are as robotic and devoid as mine. But something tells me they aren't. That's when I realize something is wrong. And just as quickly, I dismiss these newfound thoughts.

In the summer of 1983 I begin being haunted by death. The literal word "death" begins to come to me, seemingly out of nowhere: when driving the car or cooking a meal, even while watching television. The word haunts me for months. There is little I can do that is not overshadowed by this word, this thought, that sucks the joy out of any activity.

Tormented by the intrusion, I begin to feel anxious and somewhat depressed. When my friends begin to comment on my darkening mood and depression, even though I haven't shared the intrusive thoughts I've been having with anyone, I decide I need to do something to help myself out of the darkness that is taking over my daily thoughts. It's the early 1980's, and prescriptions for antidepressants are relatively unheard of. In my teen years I had dabbled in alcohol and some street drugs, but didn't enjoy the feeling they gave me. However, in the summer of 1984 I begin using a very small quantity of speed to relieve the feelings of sadness and depression that are overtaking me. By August I'm feeling better. The depression has lifted, but I begin to be concerned about using the speed as a way to cope. I know a life of using drugs to deal with the thoughts and feelings is neither healthy nor sustainable. So one night as I lay in bed, I begin to pray to God. This is a very foreign experience for me. I certainly do not know God, but I believe in Him enough to ask for His help. I pray: "God, you know me better than I know myself. I don't know why I'm doing what I'm doing taking the drugs, but whatever the reason, when it is time for me to stop, please let me know."

Later that month, still aware of the numb and depressed feelings lurking under the surface of my mind, I begin looking for help by reading the Bible. My eyes fall on the words of Matthew 7:7-8: "Ask, and it will be given to you; seek, and you will find; knock, and it will be opened to you. For everyone who asks, receives and he who seeks finds, and to him who knocks it will be opened." The words seem to jump off the page, wanting to be heard, yet I have no idea what they mean. But, for some reason, the words stick. I don't see any immediate change in my mood or any improvement in the depression, but I think I should keep reading. So, as strange as it may seem, I start reading the Bible occasionally, on top of using the speed, to help myself manage the depression and carry on with my life. For awhile anyway.

For the next eight years, always watchful of how much I'm using, I continue to self-prescribe the speed. I monitor how much I take so I won't spiral into a full-blown, unmanageable addiction. At times I stop taking it for a few days, even months at a time. The depression lifts from time to time, but as the years go by, it inevitably returns and I'm never able to shake the persistent thought of death that still haunts me.

The overwhelming dread that always follows the word "death" when it appears in my mind is persistent. It feels as if the word is the precursor to an actual death that is waiting just around the corner. I don't know where to turn or how to pull myself out of the dread that is consuming me. I don't know what I'm running from and have no idea how to escape it.

Dealing with depression and a growing sense of hopelessness during the early to mid-1980s is difficult; however, I'm able to successfully build and manage a career as an interior decorator. I also have a daughter and am doing my best to provide a happy life for her. Starting around 1986, strange and vivid images begin coming to my mind. I'm not sure what to make of them. They aren't memories, or anything that I can really describe, just flashes of something. I don't recognize any of the people in them, but that could be because the faces are not quite clear. I don't feel any emotional connections to these pictures, nor do I recognize them. I start to think they are perhaps premonitions about other people. I don't consider myself a spiritual person, but that's the only plausible, although not terribly likely explanation I can think of.

By the fall of 1988 the pictures have become clearer, but I still don't know what they mean or where they come from. I've accepted the fact that these images are just a strange intrusion in my life, and I try not to let them disrupt it. After all, who would listen to a person who claims she can see the future of the people around her?

Then one day another revelation comes to mind — a new picture. It floats into my mind, just as all the other ones in the past have. But in this one, I recognize the people who appear in it. I see a picture in my mind's eye of three people sitting in a car in a garage. My attention is caught by the fact that this picture is familiar to me. My stomach tightens, and I feel pain creeping onto the sides of my head. I recognize the garage and the car. It's the garage from a house I lived in. The image clears up, and I can see that the three people in the car are my mother, my sister and me. *This is not a vision about someone else. This is me! And I'm twelve years old. I'm in the backseat of our car, leaning over the front seat, begging my mother to let us out.* It's then that I remember the unthinkable: my mother was trying to kill us with the fumes. She wanted to commit suicide and take us with her.

The pictures continue, but none are as clear as the one I had of my mother, sister, and I. I begin to take notice of the other visions and images. I wonder what they mean? But, whenever I try to look at them, I'm stopped by an intense feeling of panic and dread. So, I do my best to not think about it and continue trying to cope with life.

About a year later I begin feeling extremely anxious and nervous. I find myself unable to sit down or relax. I always feel restless and uncomfortable.

One day as I'm having a particularly hard time dealing with the growing anxiety, I decide to take a walk. I'm secretly hoping I can outrun the fear that always seems on the verge of overwhelming me. As I walk, I try to deny the anxiety I feel. It doesn't seem to be helping, so I pick up the pace. Suddenly, I feel a sensation of electrical currents pulsing up my arms. It's like my hands have wrapped around an electric wire — both my arms feel like the nerves are vibrating. I shake my arms and try to get rid of the awful feeling. I begin to panic. *What is this?* I look around to see if perhaps I've stepped on a wire or some other live current. *Maybe an electrical tower is malfunctioning?* But there isn't a tower in sight.

Panicking, I begin to pray. I beg God to please help me. After a few minutes of desperately pleading with God and trying to get the fear under control, the feeling finally subsides. *I have to hurry home to hide! From what?* I don't know what's going on, but I think all this weird stuff that's been happening the last few years — the depression, the flashes of pictures, the anxiety, they are all beginning to pile up. I feel as though my mind is overloading, my brain is coming apart — something big is coming. *But what? What have I forgotten that's so important?*

CHAPTER TWO

I'm seven years old, sitting at the dining table with a pencil and piece of paper. I'm trying to make up a code so that I can remember my name because this family calls me Susan Elaine, but I know my name is Melanie. I use the "M" from mother and add it to Elaine to make "Melaine." I think it's close enough to Melanie for me to remember who I am. I feel proud.

May 1989

There is a movie on television tonight called *I know My First Name is Steven*. It's about a little boy named Steven who has been kidnapped. The kidnapper told the boy that his parents didn't want him any more. He said they couldn't afford to keep him, so they had asked this man to take him and raise him as his own. The kidnapper changes the boy's name to Dennis, then lies and manipulates the kid in order to gain the boy's trust and dependence.

As the movie plays, I feel myself growing more anxious by the minute. My body turns rigid and tense. I sit, frozen, too terrified to move from the couch. Something about the movie seems terribly scary to me. It's like somebody is showing a secret that shouldn't be shown. I ask Mimms to turn the TV off, and quickly. I clutch the pillow next to me. I feel like my mind is going into a panic. *What's wrong with me? Why would a movie freak me out so much?* I find myself stuck on the couch for another hour until, at last, I force myself to go to bed.

The next morning, I have no thoughts about asking myself questions that might trigger the panic again. It's like I've simply forgotten the panic I felt last night while watching the movie. But, over the next few weeks, a growing awareness creeps over me. I've never been the type of person who is over sensitive or who contemplates my emotions much, but I begin to realize that I'm not feeling anything, no emotions, nothing at all. I'm not happy or sad. I'm simply existing. An inanimate object.

The only awareness I feel is a combination of stress and nervousness. It's like my whole brain is shutting down, and the only thing left is this restlessness telling me something is wrong, terribly wrong.

Weeks later, the numbing existence has continued to eat away at my soul. I decide it's time to explore the fear that I felt while I was watching that movie. While Mimms is at work and Dana is at school, I sit down at the kitchen table, close my eyes, and breathe. I ask myself what's wrong with me. Why do I feel so anxious, yet numb? A picture begins to form in my mind. I see an open space, it's white all around me. I can go in any direction that I want, but I don't know which way to go.

I open my eyes and begin to make a list of what could possibly be wrong with me. *Why can't I feel like normal people? Well, what do normal people feel like? Maybe this is normal?* No. Normal people aren't emotionally dead. *But I'm not totally dead; I definitely feel fear. So, the real question is...why am I constantly anxious?* I hope that by a process of elimination I can find the source of my problem. I begin listing any concerns, such as finances, relationships and work. As I go through each one, I'm able to check them off. I'm not unusually worried or nervous about any of them. *Alright, apparently that's not my problem.* Then I begin to think about my husband and daughter. *Do I love them?* Without thinking, I automatically answer yes...but as I stop to think about it, I realize the answer is in my head, not my heart. *I don't FEEL anything for them, but why?* My heart has inexplicably shut down. The only thing I feel is fear. The fear is so intense now. I stop searching.

As the weeks go by, I've become vaguely aware of something gradually appearing in my mind's eye. A brick wall. *Odd. Weird. Strange.* If I shut my eyes, I can see it clearly. It's like a mental structure that is concealing something. No matter how hard I try to get past it, I cannot see what's on the other side of it. But what's even more puzzling, is that there seems to be a hole in it. The bricks seem to be coming loose and beginning to fall out. *Why is it here? How did it get here? What does it mean?*

Friday, July 21, 1989

The time is 4 am. I've just had a dream. In the dream, my mother called me on the phone and said "It's okay to talk about it now. Your dad is dead; he shot himself through the head." I begin to cry uncontrollably. I feel a dam of emotions break open, but I don't know where they're coming from. A surge of relief washes over me. Relief? A*m I relieved that I can talk about "it" now or that my Dad is dead?* I know that my father, the man who raised me, is still alive, so my feelings of relief seem odd. *Why would I feel relieved if my dad was dead?* I have no idea what the dream means. Somehow, I drift back to sleep. As I awake the next morning, life on Friday continues the same as it had on Thursday. I don't have any memory of last night's dream. It doesn't dawn on me 'til later that this is the first time in months I've been able to feel any emotion except anxiety and fear. Something has broken through.

Monday, July 24, 1989

I feel strange — almost out of body, removed from myself. I'm home alone. Mimms is out with Trey, a friend of ours who is staying at our house for a few days. I sit on the living room floor, sewing a shirt, but my mind is foggy. It's like something is going on in my brain that I am not privy to. I feel anxious, like something bad is about to happen.

I want to write something. I have something stirring in me that needs to be expressed. I lay down on the couch with pen and paper in hand. The words flow out of me, as if I know what I want to say, even though, I know nothing. I write a poem about a little girl who lives in a well. She has never seen the light of day or felt the sun upon her face. She is unwanted by the world and is kept inside the dark well all by herself. *Do I know this little girl?* The poem feels more personal than the story of some fictional, unhappy child. I can feel her loneliness, her pain. The pain she's experiencing seems to flow through me, as though I know her, and her sadness, intimately. Intuitively, I know that she's never seen the grass, or flowers or trees, nothing except the dark walls of the well where she's spent her entire life. She is all alone; her overwhelming sadness is beyond words.

The sadness and isolation of this little girl is too much for me to handle. I drop the poem and go back to sewing the shirt again. At eleven o'clock the power goes out, and all the lights go off with it. Now I am alone and in the dark. The restlessness I felt earlier matures into an all-out panic. The fear is growing, minute by minute. I'm scared. I'm hiding in the dark. *I don't know what I'm scared of. The dark, or what's in the dark?* Thankfully, Mimms and Trey arrive home soon and the power comes back on. At midnight Mimms and I go to our bedroom. I put on my nightgown and go to bed.

As soon as I close my eyes, I spring back out of the bed and start screaming, "My mom and my grandmother are after me with knives." I am running through the house trying to get away from something or someone. *Are they following me?* Mimms is there. I recognize him, but I don't really know who he is. *What's wrong with me? Why am I acting crazy?* I run to the kitchen, get in the corner and curl my body into a ball. All I can do is rock back and forth and cry hysterically.

I shut my eyes and begin to see the brick wall I had discovered months earlier in my mind falling down. Not just brick by brick, but caving in all at once. All of the nervous fear that's been building up has come crashing over me, leaving me helpless on the kitchen floor. All the death, visions, forgotten memories, physical symptoms, emotional turmoil and consuming dread have all led to this.

I need to talk to somebody. But who? Mimms is looking at me like I'm crazy. *I know; I'll call my friend, Jennie.* I look at the clock; it's 2 am. *It's late.* I decide to call her anyway. I go to the phone and call, but she doesn't answer. I'm desperate for help. I need to talk. I have to talk.

My mind is filling with memories, thoughts and fragments, quickly appearing and disappearing. I can't stop them. My brain is switching from one thought to another so quickly I can't process or focus on any of them. I see images, pictures rushing through my mind. I feel a mound of panic and confusion overwhelming me. *Where are these pictures coming from? What is happening to me?*

"There's a baby in the well," I say to no one in particular. *I have to tell someone about the baby in the well. I know the baby will die if I don't help him.* "They put the baby in the well," I scream out loud. I keep screaming about a baby in the well to our empty bedroom. I have to save the baby. *I have to tell someone. I have to save the baby.*

I decide to call Mimms' mother on the phone. She's a very patient and kind woman who'd listen to me. She picks up the receiver. "Do you know about the baby in the well?" I ask. In a very calming voice, she tells me she doesn't know about any baby in a well, but she's willing to listen if I want to tell her about it. I don't answer her; instead, I hang up the phone. *Wait. I remember. I can't save the baby now; this happened a long time ago.*

As I realize this, I run back to the corner of the kitchen and begin to rock again. A few minutes later I get up and go to the living room. I can't sit still. The more I move, the farther away I can get from all of this...I hope. Mimms, who's followed me this whole time, comes with me, but doesn't say anything. By this time Trey's awake and comes out to see what's wrong.

Suddenly, I feel an invisible whip slice across my side. "What's going on? Why are they hitting me?" I ask. I feel invisible fists raining down on my body. The blows continue, almost knocking me off my feet. I turn and look at Mimms, "What is happening to me; who's hitting me?" I feel the pain of the lashings on my skin, but I don't see anyone causing them. Then I begin to recognize the sensations; I remember that this is how it felt, being beaten long ago when I was a child. This pain *is* familiar to me.

The whipping continues. I feel the beating on my head and back. I feel a sharp pain on my temple and lashings on my legs. Mimms and Trey stand motionless, watching me being beaten by an invisible aggressor. Trey looks at Mimms.

"I think she's crazy," he whispers.

"I am NOT crazy!" I scream at him.

As quickly as it began, the beating stops. There are no scars or bruises to show the pain I've felt. Suddenly, my physical body feels strange, I feel like a little girl in a body that is too big. There's too much skin, too much height, too much room to move around in. The sensation is much like putting on very large clothes; my skin feels like it is much too big and just hanging off my bones.

I look down at my hands. I'm looking at their size, wondering why they are so big. Then I wonder what is happening to me. I look crazy. I feel crazy — but I know I'm not crazy. I am also aware that I am not in control. I know that this is not normal and I should not be acting like this. I know why Mimms and Trey are looking at me the way that they are. *I'd probably look that way too if this was going on in front of me.* Even with all that I am aware of, I'm not in control of myself. The emotions, memories and thoughts keep popping up out of nowhere and force me to go along with them. I feel like a rider on a runaway roller coaster — all I can do is try to hang on.

The chaos of emotions continue through the night. Alternating waves of fear, panic, and terror crash over me. *Where are they coming from?* I am not able to stop the madness. I have no option but to endure it.

At around 6 in the morning, Mimms has seen enough. He is freaked out and doesn't know what to do. He decides to call a psychologist that a friend of ours had once used. My friend had given me the number once when we'd had a casual conversation about child abuse. Mimms explains to the doctor what he's seen, and as best he can, what is happening, then gives me the phone. By this time I'm so confused and desperate that I am willing to talk to a stranger about all this. After a brief moment of introductions, my mind lets loose of all that it had been holding back. My life literally flashes before my eyes. Pictures are appearing in my mind like a speeding slide show. The memories start in the present and go in reverse into the past.

At first the memories are familiar. *I know these scenes.* I recognize the people, places and what I'm doing. Even though the pictures are moving so fast, I keep up with them by quickly telling the doctor what I'm seeing. *High school, friends, Matt, skiing.* The pictures keep soaring into the past, before age thirteen and now they are ALL unrecognizable! *Who are these people? What is this?* I'm drowning in fear. I can no longer describe what I'm seeing. It's so fast and unfamiliar. I have nothing to hang onto, no control. I am lost. I have an eerie feeling this is real. *It feels familiar.*

As the slide show continues, the memories reach to when I'm five years old and beyond. Suddenly everything goes black and I'm left with the expression of a "whoosh." The whoosh is both a sound and a feeling, like a span of time and space that was erased, redacted. Like I *can't* access it. The darkness that's covering it fills me with a sense of horror. The pictures come to an abrupt halt and stop as suddenly as they started. Like the light on the projector going out, my mind goes dark. I'm on the phone, still crying. I ask over and over again, "What was in the whoosh?" I repeat the question over and over. "What is in the whoosh? What's in the whoosh? I have to know what is in the whoosh." *There is something very important in the whoosh, something that I want to know, even though it seems terrifying.* My feelings contradict themselves: horror and wonder, an eagerness that something good awaits me in the darkness, but a fear of what I might find. *Can I handle what's there?*

The doctor speaks calmly to me. She tells me that I'm going to be fine and she wants to see me first thing in the morning when her office opens. She asks me if I am suicidal. I think about it for a minute, "No. I don't think I am suicidal." She asks me to give the phone back to Mimms. He writes down the address to her office and assures her that we will be there.

CHAPTER THREE

Scars are appearing on my body that I have never seen before. I start to remember how each one got there. I feel frightened and amazed all at the same time. Were they here all along? Why have I never seen them until now? I smell something rotting. I'm closed in...in...a grave?

Tuesday, July 25, 1989

Morning arrives and we are at the psychologist's office. She begins by asking me some basic questions, then quickly dives into investigating what could have precipitated the events from last night. I try my best to explain what happened the night before. I tell her I have no previous knowledge that anything is wrong, but then I add, "I have been feeling nervous." I mention the mental image of a wide open space, but not knowing which way to go, and the image of a brick wall. I tell her, "I've been searching for a reason why I've been so anxious, but I haven't come up with anything."

As I tell her this, I begin to feel small again, as if I'm in a body too large for me. I feel myself shrinking inside, like a little girl is looking through my eyes. I say, "I smell something really rotten and putrid." Neither the doctor nor Mimms can smell it, they tell me.

"What's going on? What are you feeling?" she asks.

In my mind's eye, I see a memory that emerges with the smell. "There are bugs and spiders biting me. I am in a casket with a dead body." The voice is small, quiet, and timid. I feel closed in, claustrophobic. *Was I buried alive?*

She asks me to move across the room to another chair. After I move about six feet away to a chair across from her, she asks, "Can you still smell it?"

"Yeah, I do," I say.

Seemingly out of nowhere, she then asks me who abused me when I was young. I hear a voice coming from the chair where I sit, a small voice, saying, "My mom and my grandmother." I'm so startled that I turn around and look to see who else is sitting in the chair with me. There was no one but me; the voice had come from my own mouth. *Who said that? What's happening to me?*

She asks me to describe what I am remembering. I tell her that I have been buried by the mafia after they kidnapped me. Someone had done something bad, and I was being held for ransom. I don't know what they did or why I was chosen, only that they hid me in a grave.

The rest of the appointment is spent trying to relay the information that had emerged last night. Yet when I try to explain what happened and what I saw, I can't do it. All of the memories and trauma exposed have been filed away again in the back of my head, unavailable to my conscious mind now that morning has come. All that is left are shadows and fragments of the past.

She's discussing several other things I'm no longer aware of. I'm lost in a daze, wondering what is going on. *What? When? Where did all this craziness come from?*

"Do you know what multiple personality disorder is?" she asks, interrupting my thoughts.

"Yeah, I've heard of it," I reply.

"From what I heard on the phone last night, and what I'm seeing right now, I believe you may suffer from this disorder," she explains.

"No, I don't think so," I tell her.

No longer speaking directly to me, she tells Mimms that she believes I will be safer in a hospital while I sort through these unfolding revelations.

"No way," I say. I'm terrified of institutions. I can't be locked up or drugged. *How do I know if they lock people up and drug them?*

"The only way I'll agree to go is if I can check myself in and out," I add.

After talking more about my options, and seeing that "this" is not going to get better on its own, I reluctantly begin to discuss options about staying at a facility for treatment, but only if for a small amount of time. Mimms agrees, but tells the psychiatrist he won't force me to do anything I don't want to do.

We discuss two different locations and decide on the one where I can leave any time. She assures him I can check myself out whenever I want to at this place. He agrees to take me and says we will meet her there. Still feeling claustrophobic and reeling from the revelations, I go outside the office and wait for Mimms and the doctor to finish up the details.

As he gets in the car and begins to drive, I notice that we are headed in the opposite direction from the hospital we talked about in the psychiatrist's office. In fact, it becomes clear that he's driving to the opposite facility, the one that won't allow me to check myself out once I am checked in. After I left the office, the doctor had apparently convinced Mimms that another facility was a better place to take me to than the one we had all agreed on while I was still in the room.

As we drive off, I ask, "Are we going to a different hospital than the one we agreed on?"

"No," Mimms says, "The doctor told me that this is where the one we chose is."

I'm sure it's not, but neither my opinion or my confidence level are very valuable, considering all that has been happening to me, so he continues driving to the wrong place.

We arrive a few minutes later at a psychiatric hospital. I start to cry and refuse to go in because I know this is not the place we agreed that I would go to. We argue back and forth about which facility we had agreed on in the office and where we are supposed to meet the doctor. Mimms assures me this is the place, but I'm convinced it's not. He does not believe me because of all the chaos and confusion from all of the flashbacks, but I'm completely able to understand what's going on around me. My mental sharpness is keen; my self-protection and preservation are on high alert. After a few minutes of fighting and crying, I reluctantly agree to go in.

The doctor on call at the time is here to sign me in. It's not the same doctor I saw at the office earlier. *Where she is? Why isn't she here helping me?* This doctor says he is going to take charge and asks us to follow him to a private office. As we walk, he shows me some papers he wants me to fill out. I ask him if patients can voluntarily leave after signing in for treatment. He tells me no, that I will not be able to sign myself out once I've been admitted. He says "It will take two signatures, the doctors and Mimms, for you to be released once you are committed."

I begin to panic. *No, no, I can't go in here. What are they going to do to me? I've got to get out of here.* Trying to think of a way to get out of the office and escape from this place, I calmly tell him I have to use a phone to call someone. He tells me I can use the phone on the desk in front of me. Instead, I turn and run out of the hospital. I'm not even thinking of where to go; I just want to escape. I run right into the street, in front of the passing cars. *I have to be in control; I can not be locked up.* I wrack my brain trying to figure out where I should go. *Where will I be safe? No one believes me. I can't trust anyone, not even Mimms. He's too easily swayed by their words. I have to get away.*

I stand in the middle of street, not sure what to do next. A police car begins to pass by, and I wave him down. The officer stops his car. By this time, the doctor from the hospital has caught up and is right behind me.

"Please help me. They want to put me in the hospital, and I don't want to go. My name is Susan Ruby," I tell the officer.

The policeman opens the rear car door for me, and I quickly get in. He smiles and says, "Stay in the car, and I won't let them take you."

His eyes are covered by sunglasses, so I say, "Let me see your eyes."

He pulls his sunglasses down and lets me see his eyes. *They are brown and kind. He is safe.* I tell him that his eyes are kind, so I will trust him.

The officer's eyes make me feel like I can trust him, so I decide to stay in his car. While the officer is talking with the doctor, I try to take stock of the situation. I begin to realize that I am not in control of what I'm doing. It's like my mouth, mind and body have taken over and have an agenda outside of my knowledge. *Why did I tell the cop my name is Susan Ruby? Who is Susan Ruby? What is going on here?* In spite of all the madness, I am very aware of what is going on. I just don't know why, nor do I know what this is all about. My mind is processing thoughts, making decisions, speaking names, and taking actions that I have never thought about or done before.

As I am trying to take all this in and figure out what is happening, I begin to sense another part of my mind that's making the decisions. This other part of me, the one in control — the one who calls herself Susan Ruby — is pondering my...our fate.

"Which is better," she thinks, "to be in jail or in a hospital?"

After several brief scenarios flash through my mind, she decides jail is safer. I am only privy to part of the thought process taking place. I can see pictures in my mind of the possibility of sitting in jail, but the pictures of being put in a hospital are hidden from my knowledge. Apparently this other me doesn't think I need to know what could happen in the hospital. Even though the details are hidden from me, I feel stress and panic in my body at the possibility of it. I also become aware that this "other me" thinks she is the daughter of Jack Ruby, the killer of Lee Harvey Oswald, the man who killed JFK. I am aware of the craziness of this connection, but I'm caught in this thought process nonetheless.

Finally, after a few minutes of discussion, the doctor gives up and goes back inside, leaving Mimms with the police officer. Mimms tells the officer he never intended to put me in a hospital where I couldn't check myself out, but that he was confused about what was said and where he was told to go.

The officer assures Mimms that this will all get figured out. He walks over to the car and asks, "Do you want to go with your husband?"

"Yes, but only if he lets me drive," I tell him. *I need to be in control.*

Mimms agrees to let me drive home. I step out of the patrol car and head back to our car. I cannot believe what has happened; the policeman has saved me. I don't have time to fathom at that moment what a miracle that was. I cannot imagine a police officer letting me go in the state I was in, especially against the word of professionals.

We leave the hospital and begin to head home. I'm driving well enough, but I'm not in control of my mind. My thoughts keep jumping around between the past and what's happening in the present.

As I'm driving, the picture of the brick wall appears in my mind again. Part of it has been knocked down by the memories that came flooding through last night. Now there appears to be another major breach happening. It seems as if there's another section of the wall, or another room that's been blocked off, that's collapsing.

As the thoughts come flooding through, I'm aware they are not like the memories from the night before. These thoughts are more like commands. The commands are urgent. I have to follow them, compulsively, without choice or reason. I've become a machine, programmed to carry out directives. Who gave me the directions, why are they here and what do they mean? I have no idea, but I must obey. There isn't another option available.

Suddenly, instead of heading home, my mind starts looking for the United Nations building. *The one in Switzerland?* In my mind's eye is a picture of a building that looks much like the U.S. Capitol. *I have to find it. I have to report in.* I feel panicked again, fearful of not being able to follow the command. If I don't find it, I'll be killed. *Where are these compulsions coming from? Why do I need to go there?* It seems like something that I MUST do, like breathing. You don't think about it, you just do it. I'm not sure where the building is that I need to go to. I don't think it's in Texas. *Switzerland?* The thought is intrusive, and impossible, but I know I need to find it and report in. *Report to who? For what?*

Then, without warning, I stop caring about getting to the U.N. There is a change of plans: another command. Now I need to call someone.

I can't figure out what is going on inside my brain. I know these compulsions are not normal. The thoughts just appear, like a light switch that must obey when the switch is flipped. They demand my cooperation. As soon as the directive, or command, formulates in my head, all my attention becomes focused on it and it's as if my world will end if I don't follow it. I don't have any thought process as to whether it is right or wrong, or if I want to follow the order.

I drive to a store, get out and go to the pay phone. But I just stand there; I can't remember who I'm supposed to call. I have the phone in my hand, trying to remember why I am supposed to call them. *Who is the "them"? I don't know. I know the information is in my brain, somewhere, but I can't seem to retrieve it.* Frustrated, I put the phone down and get back in the car.

I sit down in the driver's seat and stare out the window. My mind keeps fluctuating between present realities and these directives that keep popping up, but everything is happening so fast there isn't time to process or make sense of it.

By this time Mimms is a nervous wreck. He starts firing off a list of questions: "What are we doing? Where are you trying to take us? Why aren't we going home?"

I can't answer, except to tell him, "I'm looking for something or someone and it's extremely important." *I feel as though there's something I have to do, but the commands keep changing. Every time I realize I can't complete the job, the command changes.*

I know there's no way I can accurately explain all that's happening to me, so I just hope he can hold on for the ride. I feel the urge to report to some unnamed authority, so I began to drive, hoping I'll figure out where to go along the way.

As we travel down the road, I start to become paranoid. I throw anything that can be used to identify me out of the car window, including my driver's license and the contents of my purse. *All of this stuff has been given to me so that they can keep track of me. I have to get rid of everything. I can't let them find me.*

I have enough presence of mind to know I'm being paranoid, but I don't know why. It's like my brain has taken over and is giving me orders; I'm only allowed to see the actions that my mind has decided to make, not the thought process that led to them.

"I need to use the restroom," Mimms says. "Will you stop at a gas station?"

I pull over and he gets out of the car. He walks around to my window, "I'm not getting back in unless you let me drive," he says.

"Please, you have to stay with me," I plead. "If you don't, I will never see you again. I have to drive. I have to find where I need to go, but I need you to stay with me."

While Mimms walks away to think, I turn to look at the empty passenger seat. My mind becomes aware of two presences who have appeared in the passenger seat next to me. Without asking, I know exactly who they are: Samson and Delilah. Yes, the ones from the Bible.

At this moment, I am aware that I do not literally see anyone in the seat, but I sense these presences are there. I don't think they are the ghost of literal people. Rather, I believe that my mind is responding to a command: Razor blade and bridge. They are instructing me to kill myself. *Why should I kill myself? Because I remembered?* They are not speaking, but their very existence conveys their message. I know that if I can see them, then it's time for me to die. My brain associates these presences with their names, Razor Blade and Bridge, which both equate to the command to self-destruct. I don't know how I know this,

I just do. And they aren't asking, they are commanding me. I must kill myself.

I do not have a thought process available to question the logic or sanity of this message. It's not a matter as to whether I want to kill myself; rather, it is automatic, as unemotional as a traffic light when it turns from red to green. It simply has to be done.

I look back to Mimms, "Please stay with me; come with me. If you don't I will have to do what they want." I know if Mimms does not get back in the car with me, I will do what they want. I will kill myself by cutting my wrists or jumping off a bridge, probably both.

He stares at me while I beg him to get back in the car. I'm sure he thinks I'm just over-exaggerating the whole situation. Maybe he thinks if he stands there long enough, I'll snap out of this whole thing and we can go back home and be normal again, like we were before.

I don't know what changes his mind, but he finally relents and gets back in the car with me. Samson and Delilah disappear. The command to self-destruct ends as quickly as it began.

I continue driving to a new unknown destination. I am aware that I am following directions, but I do not know where the directions are coming from, or from whom. Within a few minutes, I turn onto a country road. I have never been here before. I look around to try and figure out where I've taken us. I remember seeing a map in the newspaper several months ago and slowly begin to recognize where I am. I'm driving to an occult meeting area outside of Dallas. I remember reading a newspaper article about a crime that had been committed there. I realize that I have to go here to meet someone. *I do not want to go here! This is really freaking me out. What am I doing?* I want to stop the car and turn around, but I don't. I'm not the one deciding what my body does. It's like I'm trapped inside myself. I'm a spectator to my own actions and behavior, fully aware of the craziness, but unable to stop it. Panic begins to set in.

"Susan, please stop. Where are we? Pull over and let me drive," Mimms pleads with me. I don't know if he knows where we are going, but he certainly doesn't know why. I have not told him what I have just realized. Everything is happening too quickly.

My mind starts going haywire again. I am unable to discern between the past and present. I look over at Mimms; his face looks like it is melting. *Oh my God, what is happening? I'm not drunk or on any drugs. Where are these hallucinations coming from?* Mimms is staring out the window. Then, without warning, he begins praying out loud. I'm shocked. *What is he doing? I've never heard him pray before. Does Mimms even know how to pray?* Within seconds after he starts praying, I stop the car and get out. I hand him the keys and get in the passenger seat. I can't take this anymore. I think I'm actually going crazy.

As I sit in the passenger seat, the world starts changing before my eyes. I'm not sure whether what I am seeing is in my mind or through my eyes. I see people, lots of people. They are chanting and celebrating. They pick me up and begin carrying me towards a fire. It is a celebration, a marriage ceremony. *Who am I going to marry?* Slowly the memory settles in and I remember: this is an occult meeting. They want to summon Satan for the marriage. They want to join me to Satan in marriage! I know this is a memory, not a hallucination. I am fully aware of the reality of where I actually am — riding in a car on a Tuesday morning. I'm sane.

They must have given me some sort of hallucinogenic before the ceremony, because in the memory everything is melting. All the faces and flames are curling and drooping, the colors running together.

I open my eyes and look over at Mimms, he is still melting. *He has to know what I'm seeing. Maybe he knows what to do.* I tell him about the people and the ceremony and that everything is melting. He stops the car and grabs my hand. Before I know what's happening, he's praying again, "God help us! This is the woman you have given me to love. Please help us." Within a few minutes my mind is clear — the flashback and the melting stop. I am back, fully aware, in the present.

I should be relieved because the roller coaster seems to be slowing down. Instead, fear begins creeping around the edges of my brain. For the first time, I'm able to sit back and think about where I was taking us and why. I had been obeying a command I had been given. I was supposed to bring a sacrifice to the occult. *I was bringing my husband. I was taking him to be sacrificed. This is so crazy. I need to be locked up before I hurt somebody.*

"Mimms take me back to the hospital," I tell him. "I want to check myself in. I don't want to hurt anybody." *What else am I supposed to do? I hate hospitals, but better to be locked up than risk hurting him.*

We drive back into the city and go directly to the hospital where we were this morning. We walk in to see if the psychiatrist I had met with that morning is here yet. We wait in the lobby until one of the staff members comes out. He informs us that the hospital will no longer agree to take me as a patient. He tells us to leave. More craziness. Earlier, the doctor couldn't wait to get me checked in against my will; now they won't even take me voluntarily.

Once we get home, my mind begins to calm down as the chaos of the day subsides. I go into the bedroom and lay down. I keep thinking about all that I have seen: the pictures in the slide show, the ceremony, the mental images of buildings, places, and the command to commit suicide. *Where did all of this come from? My brain has been hiding this stuff?*

As I think about it, things slowly begin to come together in my head. I remember things from old memories I've had for years that matched, or are connected to, the new memories I've been bombarded with the last couple of days. These other memories seem to add credibility to the new ones. These memories had not been blocked off behind the wall like those that flooded my mind last night; these were only long forgotten. They have been there all along, only tucked away because they were not needed.

While I lay here, my mind works as though on autopilot, connecting the pieces of the puzzle. As they are matched together, this new portrait of my life is difficult to accept. I waver, minute by minute, between acceptance and denial of what I remember. *What if my brain is lying to me? What if I am just crazy? But crazy people don't think they are crazy...but I'm open to the possibility. What else could explain all this?*

But even as I think this, I know it's not true. I am not crazy. As much as I want to deny that any of this is true, I know I recognize some of the new memories, although I don't want to. Deny, deny, deny. I don't want to be familiar with this information, these thoughts, or these things.

If all of this is true, then who does this make me? I have the strangest feeling that I've been called by a different name when I was very young. I remember sitting at a table trying to make up a code so that I could remember who I am. *Is my real name Melanie?* This memory was not been kept behind the wall of amnesia; it merely hasn't been accessed in many, many years.

CHAPTER FOUR

As the flashes of memories race through my mind, I see a second family. It seems like they had me for a short time, maybe a couple of years, more or less. Was I with them when I was 5-7 years old? The flashes of memory are swift and broken. I can't discern what each picture holds, yet I feel frightened. I'm scared to death of these people. As my mind searches for information about them, it seems like its been blocked off or kept from me. When I think of them, I feel one thing: my feet want to run and never stop. What did they do to me? The answer appears in my head — torture, just sheer torture. I feel terror at just remembering their existence.

August 1989

The scrambled memories continue to flood my brain. For days they have been revealing themselves in quickly passing pictures. Now they're beginning to slow down so that I can examine each image. Each picture or slide that I only had a glimpse of that first night is opening, but the pieces are so small I can't grasp much of what I am seeing.

Although the frequency has slowed a bit, I am still not sure what is happening. *After all these years, why is my mind letting all this through? Did it suddenly get too full? I don't know anything about flashbacks, or Satanic rituals — and I want to deny it all!* Although the memories are new, they are oddly, and scarily, familiar. I feel like I am on a roller coaster ride that I didn't choose to go on, and there isn't any way to stop it and get off. The floodgates have opened.

Since the night of the flashbacks, Mimms has stayed with me to make sure I don't have a suicidal meltdown. But time is dragging on, and I'm not getting any better. Mimms can't continue to stay home with me, but we both know that I shouldn't be left alone. We speak with Mimms' mother in Louisiana, and she suggests that we come and stay with her so she can help take care of me.

Mimms has contacts in Baton Rouge, so he can get a job. Although we really don't want to move, we both agree that it's necessary. Dana's spending part of her summer with her relatives so she can stay there and fly down to Baton Rouge after we get settled. She'll be a little late starting school, but it's the best solution we have. Mimms starts packing the house and loading our little Toyota truck for the move.

Meanwhile, I am consumed trying to figure out what is real, what happened a long time ago and what is happening now. More thoughts keep coming. Thoughts about the occult, Mafia, and other frightening people. *Who in the family owed a debt to the occult? Who belonged to the Mafia? They exchange children? They switch names and birthdates? Who am I?*

When I was on the phone with the doctor, the night of the first flashbacks, I remembered having lived with three families. Previously, I was not aware that I had ever lived with anyone but my parents. I now realize the memories of the family I had always thought were mine only go back as far as when I was around eight years old. Before that age, I don't have any memories of the mom and dad I know now.

In another flashback, I see the existence of a third family. This family goes all the way back to my birth.

The pictures and memories of them are hidden in the whoosh. But even though I can't clearly remember them, I feel loved and wanted when I think of that time. I look for the memories, but fear and denial set in. Suddenly, I have a feeling that maybe they weren't nice. *Maybe I shouldn't remember them!* My heart and mind are battling between the emotional contradictions I feel about this family. Familiarity and love, fear and panic. *I think I've been told they didn't want me, just like the boy I saw in the movie. Did they do that to me too?* My mind quickly shuts off the recall, as if I'm not allowed to think about them. I feel a struggle in my soul: were they good — or were they bad? *I want to know either way. I want to know about them. I have to find them, I have to tell them I am alive. No, they are evil. There isn't a family to find. There isn't a family to tell. There isn't anything to tell. You're crazy.* My mind battles between the thoughts.

As we continue to pack for Louisiana, I'm still pre-occupied by thoughts about that third family. They lived on a farm too. As I think about and process the memories of the other two families, I no longer feel afraid of the third one. I think I was tricked or manipulated into being fearful of them. My mind seems bent on finding them. *I think I am from the northeastern United States, possibly New York or Massachusetts.* I scour the map looking for names of towns I might recognize. *Portsmouth? No. Troy or O'Fallen? No. I'm confusing the places again. I can't remember.*

I try to remember my last name. *It's too long. I never learned to write it because it was too long.* I try to remember the mother's name. I can't. I begin to feel desperate to find them. *I want to tell them that I am alive. I want to tell them that I remember them. I want to tell them I am sorry I couldn't find them sooner.* I feel sad about the lost years. *I wonder if they looked for me. Did they try to find me?*

As we drive from Texas to Louisiana, I continue having moments of paranoia and crying. One minute I feel almost normal, then I feel paranoid. *Someone is going to come and find me. I didn't do what I was supposed to do. No, no one is looking for me. That was all a long time ago.* My emotional awareness is wavering between the past and present. Even as I try to process the information, I worry that my mind might betray me again. *I don't know what caused the avalanche of memories or how to stop if it happens again. I am scared of them, I'm scared of me.*

After we cross the border into Louisiana, I find myself looking at the scenery with new eyes, as if I've never been outside before. The colors are so vivid and bright. I feel amazed at the beauty of the sky, the trees and the fields. Everything seems new and exciting. I notice that I am looking at each farmhouse we pass, searching for one that is two-story with a porch across the front, white with black shutters on the windows. In my heart, I know I'm looking for my home. I remember another time and place — one that doesn't scare me. It's familiar and unfamiliar all at the same time. I feel like I am a little girl again. *I want to find my way home*. Pictures of an attic bedroom with wicker furniture wander through my mind. I feel safe in the memory. I think I was loved there. I feel safe on the farm I see in my head.

We arrive in Louisiana to a warm greeting from Mimms' family. We have settled in and within a couple of weeks Mimms begins working for a local construction company. His mother, Gerri, works part time, so she is able to stay at home with me quite a bit. She listens to me talk and process my memories, which is helpful. I am beginning to unravel the mystery, piece by piece. I feel infused with a sense of pride and purpose that I am finding my way through the maze.

I begin to gain a lot of clarity in regards to the flashbacks, but that clarity becomes hard to hold on to. Whenever I hear conversations or information from current news or present-day subjects, my thoughts become easily influenced. I mix up the past with the present. I begin to doubt what actually happened in my past versus what was just discussed in the news. I can't find the answers I'm searching for. I'm so confused. All I feel is defeat and humiliation.

I had hope. But now, will I ever find my way? Will I ever be normal? I was so hopeful of remembering who I am and where I come from, but now I am just confused. I think my real mother's name is Kitty and that I always named my cats "Kitty," as a way to remember her. But now, I'm not sure. Some guy named Dukakis is running for president and his wife is named Kitty. *Is she my mother? They are from Massachusetts!* Gerri keeps talking about someone else named Kitty, too. *Is that why I think my mother's name is Kitty?* I don't know. I'm lost. How could I think I was a child of a presidential contender? How stupid am I?

I decide to try and get answers from another source besides my brain. I call my mother, then my father — the ones I remember growing up with from 8 years old — and ask them about some of the details I am remembering.

They both deny any knowledge of anything unusual in my childhood. At this point, after all of the craziness that's happened to me in the past few weeks, I don't believe them. *Maybe they want to keep the information from me. Were they involved? How could they not be involved? How could they not know anything?*

After speaking with my mother, then my father, and getting nowhere, I decide to call my sister. She answers the phone and I delve right in, telling her I've been having some strange memories and want to see if she can help me make sense of them. She says, "Sure, I'll see if I can help you."

I ask her if she remembers me being crazy when we were little. (I have a mental picture of me as a child frantically pacing in circles as if I were going mad.) She answers, "No." Then I ask her if she remembers a time when I didn't live with them. She becomes very upset and starts screaming.

"You can't talk about this; you can't remember. They just killed three people up the road the other day. You are going to get us killed. Don't you ever call me again." She is panicked, screaming, and pleading with me to stop asking questions.

As she yells, I keep trying to tell her, "I did remember what happened, and I didn't die. It's ok to remember. I DID, and I lived through it."

I'm not sure if she heard me. She slammed down the phone. She was so scared. I wonder what's happened to her? Just a few years before, she and my father had moved back to the area where we lived when these things happened. *I wonder what she knows.* I'm not sure who did these things and I don't know who she was talking about that was killed, but I decide to cut off all contact with my entire family to protect me, and them. *If they want to be in denial, fine. I know something.* But part of me is afraid she might be right. *Will they kill me now that I remember?*

I'm sitting in a chair in the dining room. I look down at my legs. I notice they have small scars all over them. They look like recent, fresh scars. They are very red and look as though they've just finished healing. I'm in the grave. It's dark, hot and stinky. Bugs and spiders are crawling all over me. I can't move. *Am I too afraid to move? Or is it too crowded? Why is it crowded? Another body?* The memory of where the bites came from appeared in my minds eye. Just as the memory unfolds, my mind snaps back to the present. It's too much for now. Although it happened many years ago, I see the marks for the first time. I know this is a continuation of the same memory I had in the doctors office where I first remembered that smell.

I see another small scar underneath my right forearm and several more scars on the tops of both my arms. There is another fresh-looking scar on my left wrist, going lengthwise along the main vein. I can even see the holes where the stitches were. *Did I do this to myself?* As I ask myself the question, I see someone showing me how to do it — the memory. They are teaching me how to self-destruct, commit suicide, rather than remember or reveal what they have done to me. They cut my wrist with a straight razor: a long handle with a razor in it. They are very neat and tidy. *They must have cut along the side of the vein because there isn't much blood.* Then they stitch it up and wrap a gauze bandage around it. The people are acting very calm and matter of fact, as if they are teaching me how to sew a piece of cloth. Then, another memory comes...I remember that two years after they showed me how to do this, while I was in junior high, I'd been afraid to play volleyball because I thought I would split my wrist open if I hit the ball.

As I sit here, my body is revealing more information that's been hidden. I see more scars appearing. It seems like my body is legitimizing what my mind has been telling me: I've been through uncountable tortures and abuse. But still, I want confirmation, so I turn to Mimms.

I ask him to come over to where I am sitting. "Do you see anything on my legs, arms or wrists?" I ask.

"Yeah, I can see scars," he says and points at the ones on my wrists. He adds, "But I haven't ever seen them before."

"Are you sure you see these?" I ask again. I need reassurance that I am not crazy.

"Yeah," he says, as he starts pointing to each one along my arms, legs and wrists.

I feel relieved that I am not hallucinating; however, I wonder where the scars have been all these years. *Why couldn't they be seen before now? What else has my mind and body kept from me? How can this happen? How did my mind just decide on its own to keep secrets from me? And then how did it decide when to reveal them? Why reveal the secrets now?* My denial was beginning to crumble.

I obviously have very little control over what's happening to my body and mind. I secretly wondered if "control" was just an illusion I let myself have for comfort, and that it might disappear at any time. After all, the memories in my mind and body seemed determined to make themselves known, with or without my approval.

It's the assurance that my husband believes in me that helps me through these early days. Even though I feel myself gaining mental strength back each day, it's mostly two steps forward and one back. I often vacillate between acceptance and denial of each new revelation that comes. As I struggle through each new wave of information, I realize it will take years to reveal, and unravel all that I saw that first night. And even longer to understand what I saw. Even so, my mind goes back to the same thoughts over and over again. *What did they do to me? Why did they do it?*

I've begun seeing a local psychologist who is a friend of Mimms' family here in Baton Rouge. Margaret Periboom is a gentle, elderly woman with a psychology practice that helps people with fairly minor issues. Since I started seeing her, I've told her what happened during the flashbacks and what memories I've had since then.

I also tell her about incidents I think happened to my friends when I was a teenager. I remember beatings, accidents, and abuses; friends who had been abused or traumatized by their fathers. However, I soon realize that I had been beaten, too and that I had used my friend's identities as a way to store my painful memories. When I was beaten, I remembered instead, that it happened to one of them.

"The doctor I saw in Texas told me she thinks I have multiple personality disorder," I tell her.

"I've made a list of names of my friends who I thought were beaten, but now I realize that it was me. My father was beating me."

"I wonder if this is just a list of names, or the names of personalities?"

"What do you think?" I ask her.

She replies that she isn't familiar with the disorder, but she doesn't seem shocked by my revelation. She says she would like for me to continue seeing her and we can explore it together.

We continue to meet twice a week. I feel I can trust her. She is easy to talk to and has a kind spirit about her. At my appointments I talk about all that I've been remembering. I'm making progress, although at times I still feel like a newborn baby trying to stand for the first time — I'm shaky, at best. It's hard to piece the past together after having my life turned upside down.

As I go through the process of sorting out the memories, I've begun having incredibly vivid dreams. There is something about them that seems so real. I think more memories are leaking through into my dreams. When I wake up, I know more about what happened than the dream showed me. *I remember. I really remember.*

One night after I wake up from a dream, I go into Mimms' mother's room. I wake her up and tell her about it. It was about witches. There were dark places, meetings, people doing strange things.

"Do you know that there are such things as witches?" I ask, testing her.

Half awake, she sits perched on the edge of her bed. "Yes," she answers, "I know there are witches."

"Do you know they do bad things to little kids?" I ask.

I don't wait for her to answer. *I've said too much. Panic.* Instead, I tell her I have to go back to bed. I feel relieved that she believes in witches, but I am not sure I want to tell her any more about them. I feel paranoid. *Maybe...she's a witch.*

One day shortly after that, I'm at my meeting with Dr. Periboom, and I decide to mention witches and the occult to her.

"Have you ever heard about witches?" I hesitate...then add, almost whispering, "Do you know what they do to children?"

I don't know if she answered. I blocked it out. The look on her face and in her eyes tell me her thoughts: shock and disbelief. *I've made a mistake. She doesn't believe me.* Mild panic begins to set in. I excuse myself and get up to leave. I don't know if my hour is up, but I leave anyway.

She thinks I'm crazy. Now I will be put away in a home for crazy people. Normal people don't know about witches or the occult. I can't talk about these things. What am I going to do? I need help, but I can't tell. I have so much to tell, but no one will believe me.

The trust we had built was quickly washed away with the look I saw in her eyes and on her face.

At our next meeting she asks me to see a colleague of hers, a psychiatrist. She explains it is just to make sure she is "on the right track." What she really means is "I need to see if you are crazy." I hide my reluctance and agree to go. She makes the appointment for me. *I'm not crazy, but that doesn't matter if she thinks I am.*

I see the psychiatrist, and he asks me several simple questions.

"What day of the week is it?" he asks.

"Wednesday," I answer.

"Who is the U.S. president?"

"George Bush."

"Tell me something that happened a few days ago."

He just wants me to name something, anything. I don't want to be labeled crazy, so I answer with what seems to me to be perfectly normal responses. Part of me wants to be sarcastic with my answers just to let him know that not only am I NOT crazy; I'm also not an idiot. *You'd have to be dead to not be able to answer these questions, not crazy.* But I behave myself and pass the sanity test. As I get ready to leave, he tells me I'm fine and he will send a report back to my doctor. *Well, that's a relief. I've been declared sane by merely knowing what day of the week it is!* By this point, I'm not crazy; I'm angry.

At my next appointment, Dr. Periboom says that the psychiatrist has encouraged her to proceed with me as she had been. But, now the trust I had with her is broken.

I know I am not crazy, but I also know how crazy all of this sounds...but what am I supposed to do? I want to trust her, but how can I? If she has trouble when I talk about witches, how will she believe anything else I tell her? I know, somehow in my gut, these memories are just the tip of the iceberg. *How can I go on uncovering the past if I risk being labeled insane every time I open my mouth?*

I decide it's better to be seen as sane than continue to figure out what's been going on with me. So, I withdraw. I stop processing memories. I quickly descend into denial and complacency. I continue with our sessions for a short while longer. I tell her there is nothing new to talk about and that I am fine. In truth, I am far from fine. I'm still discovering new information about my past, but I keep it to myself. I don't talk about it with anyone, not with Mimms' mother or Dr. Periboom. I decide to ignore it — and it will go away. Deny, deny, deny!

"We are moving back to Dallas since I am doing so much better now," I tell her as we are sitting in her office one day.

I can see by the look on her face she's skeptical, but what can she say?

"Thank you for helping me," I say as I shake her hand goodbye. I don't know where else to turn, and I don't have the courage or the strength to look for someone else, so I promptly put her and all the memories back in the past where I hope they stay.

I am stronger now and I can once again take care of myself, so we don't need to remain in Baton Rouge any longer. In November we move back to Texas and start over.

We rent a little house in the city. The winter passes uneventfully. Mimms goes back to work at the same job, and Dana is in school. I have a part-time job. Life is back to normal, or as normal as it can be since my discoveries eight months ago.

From time to time my thoughts still wander to the flashbacks, but most of the time I don't think about them very long before I change the subject in my mind. I know I haven't fully regained my mental strength. Sometimes I secretly worry that my mind will betray me again. *It did it once; it might do it again.* Since I have stopped trying to put the pieces of the puzzle together, I try to live each day with caution, trying to keep my life balanced, with lots of rest and no stress. I worry that stress might cause another mental avalanche — and I might not survive it a second time.

Dallas, Spring 1990

It's a Saturday evening in April of 1990. Dana is visiting her father's family for the weekend. Mimms and I have been visiting friends in Fort Worth. We arrive home at about 2 am and notice the light we left on inside the house is not on anymore. Mimms opens the door and tries to flip on another light, but nothing happens — the house remains black. We step inside and realize the whole house is black because of smoke. The smoke is so thick we can't even see our hands. The house has been on fire. I go next door and call the fire department. When we get back inside, we try to find our cat, Kitty. We find Dana's hamster in his cage, but we can't find Kitty. When the firemen arrive, they tell us to go outside while they search the house for the cause of the fire and make sure it is completely out. One of the firemen finds Kitty under our bed. She is unconscious. He brings her outside and gives her oxygen to revive her. She begins breathing again, but she needs medical attention. We leave the firemen at the house and take Kitty to a veterinarian hospital, taking the hamster with us. We have a sick hamster, a cat that is need of emergency medical care, a hundred dollars, and the clothes on our backs. *I wonder if they have found me? Did the evil people do this?* So much for remaining stress free.

The next morning we meet with the captain of the fire department. He says the ice-maker in the refrigerator caused the fire. *It wasn't even connected or turned on, yet it had somehow exploded, leaving a gaping hole in the side of the freezer?* The explosion had blown the cabinets off the wall, out the kitchen window, and into the yard.

He said, "The fire burned for approximately two hours until it burned itself out because of a lack of oxygen. I'm surprised it didn't reignite, causing a backdraft, when you opened the front door and let in more air." He added, "I've been a fireman for twenty-three years, and I've never seen a refrigerator or ice-maker explode before."

I try to not let my mind wander, but the thought slips in: *Was this a warning? Are they watching me? How does an ice-maker blow up by itself?*

He tells us the smoke is very toxic — it has the potential to cause serious illness — and we shouldn't try to save anything from the house. *The smoke permeated everything. There isn't anything to save.* I feel scared as I look around and see what happened in the house. The most disturbing sight is Kitty's paw prints. She had looked everywhere for a way out. I can feel her desperation. There was no where to go, no where to hide. Her tracks are in the ash on the floor as she went door to door, and window to window, looking for a way to escape until she finally collapsed while trying to hide under our bed. I am devastated. The thought that she was trapped and I was not there to help her is devastating. Guilt covers me. My mind has other thoughts, too, creeping in ever so slowly: *There's no where to hide; there's no way out.*

Sunday afternoon I go by the animal clinic where we left her the night before. I'm allowed to go in and visit her, but I can't hold her because they are giving her oxygen. She can barely lift her head, but her eyes open slightly and she sees me. My heart and mind are breaking. *I can not look at her. She was trapped and helpless, and I know too much about what that feels like.* I can't stay long because I feel the stress and anxiety building in my body. The emotional similarities are rising to the surface. *I have to leave. Now.*

Later that night, the doctor calls and tells me that Kitty isn't doing well and has taken a turn for the worse. He suggests we have her put to sleep.

"It will take months inside the oxygen tank for her to recover, if she recovers at all," he says.

Mimms and I know we can not financially afford to keep her there, so we agree. I would never admit this to Mimms, but I know I cannot afford the emotional cost either. I need to cut my losses to try to keep myself together. I have to choose where to focus my energy. I choose myself over my cat. Sadness and guilt are my companions in this crime of selfishness.

The first few days after the fire, a few neighbors come by to ask what had happened when they see us cleaning out the house. They didn't know there had been a fire until they saw the fire truck at our house Sunday morning. *I can't understand how a fire — and explosion — could have burned for more than two hours, and no one saw or heard anything.*

We finish cleaning out the house and go through what is left of our belongings. We have to wear masks over our nose and mouth because the fumes and ashes are toxic. The walls, floors and furniture are burnt black and covered with ashes. A couple of friends come by and help us carry the contents of the house out to the street for the garbage men to haul off.

The smell is not like I would have imagined. This smells of plastics, chemicals and wood. It is eerie being in the house. I feel nervous all day...like the house is taunting me. *Was this a freak accident or have they found me? Do they know I remember? Was my sister right — will they try to kill me?*

We manage to save a Bible that was a wedding gift, one bed frame and a side table. They have the least amount of damage and I think they can be saved. (I find out later that the smoke was like liquid. It continued to ooze out of the wooden table and bed frame for years.) The landlord's insurance policy doesn't cover our personal belongings since it's a rental house, and we don't have our own policy. We have no clothes, no home and no money. We have to start over, again.

We stay with friends, and other friends begin bringing us food and clothes. The following weekend they hold a benefit for us that raises over $1,200. Within two weeks we are able to rent an apartment. We still don't have furniture, but after a few weeks we are given a bed, a couch, dishes, pots, pans and all the necessities. I can't help but see that we are very blessed to have generous, caring friends.

The stress — and threat — of the fire has caused a rumbling just below the surface of my mind. I am secretly worried about another avalanche of flashbacks. *I only know bits and pieces from the first ones...is there more?* I feel pressure mounting on the sides of my head, like a vice grip squeezing my forehead and temples. I take extra care not to let my mind wander.

One afternoon, about a week after moving into our new apartment, the phone rings. It's an old friend. She says my sister called her with a message for me. My grandmother, my father's mother, has died. She was a warm, loving woman who made me my favorite foods and prayed with me at bedtime. She was always kind, and I had fond memories of her. Even after I was an adult, she never forgot to send a gift or card for my birthday or Christmas. I don't know where she fits into the new-found memories that have intruded on my life. But, I am sure of one thing: she was a bright light. Of all that I remember, I feel sure of her love for me.

April 1990

With the fire and the death of my grandmother and cat happening so close together, my ability to remain stress free has come to an abrupt halt. The memories are still haunting my mind. *What about the witches? What about the occult? I wonder if the fire had been a threat. Maybe someone found out that I remember.* Even as I have these thoughts, I can't help but wonder. *What did they do to me? I don't know.* But I can feel something lurking, once again, in the back of my mind.

The memories are pressing in again, and as much as I fear the unknown, I am also cautiously curious. I still don't know anything about the subject of multiple personalities, so I begin by praying, asking God to please help me. I figure if there is anyone who can help me, it will be Him. I slowly ask Him for the truth. I tell Him that I need to know what is in my past. I want, need to be free from this haunting. *I can't continue being scared of my mind, or the past.*

I decide I should re-examine the memories from last year. I begin by thinking about the night before the flashbacks started — how eerie and scared I felt all evening. *I don't like the feeling I had that night, and I don't want to think about it.* Quickly, I fast forward to the events that unfolded while I was on the phone with the doctor. As I do, my mind goes off on its own. I see a visual image in my head of a toy box blown open, the hinges of the lid are barely hanging on. The toys (my memories) are mixed up, damaged, unrecognizable. It's as though Barbie's head is on Ken's body; the wheels of a toy truck are attached to the body of a stuffed animal. All the sensible structures are gone. The toys are strewn throughout the room, and none of it makes sense. *I think that's a good description of what happened that night...It's gonna take years to make sense of this mess.* I feel like I am facing an impossible task. I want to solve the mystery or at least put the toys back in the box, but I am overwhelmed by the unknown. I don't even know where to start. *What do I do with this mess? Where do I start?*

Small bits of memories are coming almost daily. I gather my notes from last year's memories and add my new notes, hoping to find a way to put the puzzle together. *I don't like long projects, or puzzles, so let's wrap this up quickly.* I draw a timeline and place the memories in the years they happened in an attempt to build a chronological map of my life. I soon realize that before age thirteen there are many things that don't fit, just as in the flashbacks. Before age thirteen my life becomes unrecognizable. It's like two person's lives are intertwined, overlapping each other many times. Some memories take place at times when I should have been in school. Yet if these memories are correct, I can't be in both places. *Could some of these just be pictures I have seen? Can I actually place myself in the memory and look around and find more details?*

One day I am sitting on the bed going over my notes. As I am fighting for the truth, a memory surfaces that makes my head feel dizzy. *I have a twin sister.* The thought makes me feel sick. I banish it from my mind. *I don't want this.* Denial tries to protect me. *I'm not prepared.*

When the thought persists, and my denial crumbles, I commit myself to finding reasonable explanation for the twin. *Is it possible that having multiple personalities would explain the memories that are unfamiliar to me? And the twin? Maybe she is another personality?* I keep looking for an acceptable answer. *But that doesn't explain the double timeline that occurs. I cannot have two sets of memories for the same place in time!* The memories battle back and forth, each one trying to take precedence over the other. *Which ones are true? Which ones are fake? If some are false, how did they get here? How does a person get memories that aren't true? That can't be right.*

A revelation occurs to me. Many of my memories, the ones I had always thought were real, are nothing more than photos or movies I was shown, stories I was told. I can not draw out any more information about them other than the original story that has repeated itself in my mind, like a recorded message. *If it is me in the pictures, shouldn't I at least remember who took the photos or if I posed for them? Where did the pictures come from? Where have I seen them?*

As my questions persist, my thoughts move me to a new place. I see a dark room appearing. I am standing in front of a movie screen. There is a movie playing on the screen. Someone in the movie looks just like me! She's learning to ride a bike. Someone else is telling me a story. *That's me on the bike? How can I be on the bike? I'm here.*

I quit thinking. *I have to stop.* I bring my mind back to the present. I get up and move around the room. *I've had enough for today.* My mind feels like it's swimming, like I'm caught in an ocean. I can't find the shore fast enough. I feel panicked. *I have to stop these thoughts.*

CHAPTER FIVE

I see a woman with multiple personalities on the Oprah show today. Her face seems to be wincing as she tells her story. I see the stress and pressure around her eyes and forehead. Her whole posture is changing as she speaks. I sense what she's feeling; I, too, feel pressure on my temples and can barely keep my eyes open when the memories are pressing in on me.

May 1990

S ince I saw Trudy Chase, the woman with multiple personalities, on the Oprah show, I feel certain that the doctor in Texas was right to diagnose me with multiple personalities. There are many similarities in our stories. For example, when the memories first emerged, I created a list of people that I knew growing up that had been abused. I knew how they had been abused, and most of the time I could guess by whom. However, as I delved through the memories, it began to dawn on me that perhaps these names weren't real people at all. They could be names of files or personalities that were created to contain the memory of that abuse.

The days of discovery have begun again. Only this time I am not being flooded with information like I was before, nor am I stuck in denial, at least I don't think I am. I really think I am ready to know the truth. I have been praying, asking God to guide me and show me what is true and what isn't. I still feel fragile, mentally speaking, but I want to go forward. I've found the name of a psychologist at the local mental health agency. I've made an appointment to see her.

At my first session with the counselor, we exchange pleasant greetings. Privately, I think she looks too young and inexperienced, especially compared to Dr. Periboom, who was close to retirement. But I have nothing to lose and nowhere else to go, so I begin to tell her about the memories I have recovered so far. I tell her about the grave and the scars appearing. I tell her that I think I am someone else — my real name is Melanie. She seems to accept what I tell her. I inch forward relaying all that I remember...everything except the occult and witches. I withhold this bit of information out of fear that she will think I am crazy too.

"I feel stress in my back and head. I also feel pressure on the sides of my head and get dizzy sometimes when I remember some things. Is that normal?" I ask her.

"Yes," she assures me. "Those are very normal feelings. Your trauma and memories have been blocked so long they want to be released."

Each week I go to my appointment and pick up where I left off the previous week. The pressure I feel in my temples always return as I talk about my memories.

"Do you feel angry?" she asked one day.

"No, I don't," I reply. Since the emotional roller coaster had been unleashed with all the memories, I'm not sure how I feel, *but I don't think I'm angry.*

Her question stays in my mind for days. I think about my feelings, my emotions. *I know I feel things now that I've never felt before. It's not that I haven't ever felt emotions, but I feel them stronger now, like after the first memories when my eyes saw colors in the world more vibrantly, as if I was seeing them for the first time. I wonder if I've been feeling "filtered" emotions all my life*. As this realization sinks in, I feel queasy. *Can this really happen?*

"Did my mind filter my memories **and** my emotions?" I say aloud to an empty room. Thinking back on the doctors question, I think — betrayed, I feel betrayed by my own mind. That's how I feel!

Although I'm grateful for the sanity, I can't help but feel grieved because my mind hid the truth from me. I know it was for my survival, but I still feel betrayed. The life I remember before last year was fairly normal, but it wasn't the truth. The truth was unacceptable. *I am angry.* So many years ruined and wasted on lies and half truths. *My mind. I suppose I'm angry at my mind. It betrayed me. I don't care that it was for my survival. How can I ever trust it again?*

After several weekly visits to the psychologist, I've recounted all the memories that I've already had time to adjust to, then I begin reciting the places I've lived, how long I lived in each house, and the schools I've attended. I go over the memories from the July flashbacks, the same ones I had discussed with Dr. Periboom. I begin noticing that I keep returning to this same basic information, as if I'm subconsciously reluctant to go deeper into my past... especially before age thirteen. I know I must sound like a robot; there's no depth or emotional connections to what

I'm telling her. They're just words — prerecorded messages — not memories.

Why can't I go any further? Just thinking about that question scares me. It takes me awhile to realize that to go further means I'll be going into unknown territory. *Can I survive if what I learn is worse than what I already know?*

I feel certain that this doctor is not the right one to help me. *She seems so innocent. I need to talk about things that she will not understand, it will be too much for her to hear.* If I remember the past, I know darkness is there, waiting, and I'm going to be scared. I need someone who can help me who won't be scared too.

At my next appointment, I tell her my concern: "I think I'm ready to talk about some of the stuff that happened before I was thirteen, but I'm worried you won't be able to handle it. I'm worried it'll scare you off."

She tries to reassure me, "Susan, I will be ok. I'm here and willing to listen and help."

I still feel like I can't tell her. I don't really know why I can't. Maybe she would be ok. Maybe I am just procrastinating.

Although she has assured me that she is willing, I still end our sessions just two months after they began. As I drive away from her office, I pray and ask God to bring the right person, soon. *I am not sure how long I can hold off whatever is pressing in on me.*

August 1990

By the end of August I have not found a new counselor. One Saturday morning I happen to see an advertisement in the newspaper for a conference for psychologists who work with multiple personality patients. The guest speaker is Trudy Chase, the woman I had seen on the Oprah show. I can hardly believe it. I call the phone number for the conference, and they say that it's for doctors, but the public is welcome to attend — and it is free. "It starts in thirty minutes," the receptionist says.

I arrive just after the meeting starts. The room is full of people associated with the mental health profession, in one way or another. *Boy, do I feel out of place. But, I'm desperate.* I'm the only non-professional in the room, other than the guest speaker. I've no idea what to expect or what they will talk about, but I want to listen and learn. *Maybe I will find someone to help me.* They are talking about the clinical side of the process: how and why personalities are formed, their function, and how multiple personalities help the core person survive the trauma. Ms. Chase tells her story. She knows how her personalities developed and functioned. She relates the traumatic abuse she suffered at the hands of her father. As she talks I can, again, see the subtle changes in her face and body that I'd seen months earlier on TV.

When the meeting ends, I go to the front to talk with her. I introduce myself and ask her if she has time to talk.

"Yes," she replies. "That's why I'm here." She seems genuinely open and available.

I start right in, anxious to get some answers. "I've been going through memories of my childhood, and sometimes I feel pressure on my temples and other places. When you were talking, I thought I saw the same thing happening to you. Do you feel that?"

She answers, "Yes, that's what happens when I switch from one personality to another or when a memory is pressing in."

I tell her, "I started having flashbacks last year, and I've been looking for help."

Ms. Chase introduces me to another person who has been listening to our conversation. "This is Dr. Teresa; she's a psychologist who works with survivors of SRA."

"What's SRA?" I ask.

"It stands for Satanic Ritual Abuse," the doctor replies.

I can't believe my ears. I've never heard of SRA, but I certainly have memories about the occult and witches.

I've been keeping them to myself since mentioning them to Dr. Periboom. *Now's my chance to get help.*

I ask the psychologist, "Do you think you can help me? I've had memories about witches and the occult."

"But I don't have insurance" I add.

"That's okay," she replies. "Here's my card. Just call the office and the receptionist will make an appointment for you. We can set the fee based on what you can afford."

She hands me her card, and I put it in my purse. A wave of relief and excitement washes over me.

I rush home and tell Mimms about my day: "I've actually found someone who will understand my memories and help me — and the fee is based on what we can afford!"

"I doubt they will help when they find out what we can afford to pay," he says.

"I have nothing to lose, Mimms. Monday I'm going to call and make an appointment."

Monday can't come fast enough. I call first thing in the morning and tell the receptionist the name of the doctor I met on Saturday. I also tell her I don't have insurance to pay for the visits. She asks if I mind seeing one of their new associates, Mrs. Jean Ann Dixon.

"No, I don't mind." *I'm just anxious to get started.*

"She's getting her license and does her internship at our office," the receptionist says. "You can see her right away, how about Thursday at five?"

"Sure, I'll be there." I am so excited to finally start sorting through the scattered pieces of information that have been pressing on my brain for months.

Thursday finally comes and I arrive at the psychologist's office right on time. Jean Ann is a very soft-spoken, pretty woman in her early forties. She tells me she's getting her license to practice psychology, and I'm one of her first patients. She tells me she's eager to learn from me. *Well, at least she's eager rather than nervous.* At our very first meeting, I show her my notebook in which I've written the discoveries I've made so far. I boldly tell her some of the things I want to discuss: witches, the occult and programming — the compulsive need I felt during the flashbacks to find the occult ground and the United Nations and to commit suicide. *I watch her reaction when I bring up all of these subjects. I need to know if she can accept that these things really exist.*

"Do you know that witches and the occult really exist?" I ask. I wait to see some doubt or hesitance pass over her. She doesn't show any shock or disbelief anywhere, not on her face or in her eyes.

"Yes, I know they do," she says. "My work here has made me familiar with these and MPD (Multiple personality disorder)."

She adds, "I want to learn from you. You will do most of the work. I am here to listen."

This definitely helps relieve some of the nervousness I am feeling, but I need to be certain she understands that I don't want to be pushed.

"I don't want you to use hypnosis, and I need to look at the memories at my own pace. I need to be in control about whatever comes up in our discussions. No surprises."

She agrees and is willing to work with me in whatever way I'm comfortable. That evening I go home with renewed hope.

Over the next two years, Jean Ann proves herself to be a kind, patient and understanding counselor. We meet each week for an hour. In addition to my weekly sessions, I start attending meetings for persons with multiple personalities. The group meetings are supposed to be good for me because I can meet other people with multiple personalities. However, I find that I don't really have much in common with most of them. Many of the people in the group have sorted through their memories and seem to have everything wrapped up neat and tidy. I also dislike the fascination they seemed to have with MPD. It seems to me that they find it almost entertaining. They speak of ritual abuse as though it has been a privilege or honor. They tell stories about each personality having their own clothes and friends and how the occult gave them special attention and called them princesses. One person says she was given a pet seal by the occult. In my opinion, they don't seem to be genuine or traumatized.

There is one young lady, Laurel, who is really having a hard time with recovery. She speaks of having a twin when she was young. Her twin was killed by the occult when she was ten or eleven years old. I still have not let my mind ponder the memory of my twin but, her story catches my attention. I am actually encouraged because of the similarities. Not many people think they have a sibling who was killed by the occult, and although I've not fully accepted having a twin yet, at least I know I wouldn't be the only person that it ever happened to. Even though I remember seeing a twin, and can even tell you how she was killed, I still deny there was a twin immediately after telling you how she was killed. That is the level of my denial. However, after hearing her story, I feel I can be brave enough to explore my own memory and not feel insane. I have gained some things by attending the group meetings, but I eventually decide not to continue. I feel like I am comparing my level of recovery and sanity based on theirs. Overall, it isn't helpful.

Jean Ann and I are making progress, but I have a problem, a big one. Information is coming out, but nothing we can piece together. I feel as though I am chasing ghosts, and I'm not being healed. It's like a BIG surgery incision that just won't heal — a big gaping wound filled with infection. I'm trying to sort through the mess of information and I have gained some perspective, but I just can't get over the trauma. Mentally, I'm still haunted and in shock that all these thing happened, and I didn't even know about it. I often return to the same thought: *How could my mind betray me like that?* I wonder, and worry, again and again, if I can ever trust myself?

The list of names of personalities is growing. The number is overwhelming, and I am getting worse. Emotionally, mentally, and spiritually, I am a mess. I recognize and understand how the personalities function, all the years keeping my secrets and allowing me to retain my sanity. But now, when they reveal their life story, I am left in a whirlwind of emotions and confusion.

This new reality is hard to reconcile with my existence. What do I do with this new view of the world, my world? Where do I put all this? I don't have a file for it. I don't even know how to make one. Label it crazy and put

it in the basement? Apparently, my mind did that once...
didn't work!

I'm unwilling for the personalities to be exposed during my sessions with Jean Ann. I feel the need to protect them as they once protected me. I do not want them, or me, to become a circus act. Maybe I feel ashamed. Maybe I feel embarrassed.

I don't delve into who has which friends, the clothes they choose to wear, or other differences. We're all working towards the same goal: being free from trauma and being healed. If any one of the personalities has something to say, they say it through me. The psychology world refers to a person like me as a high functioning MPD, meaning that, as an adult, I haven't had lapses in time. I'm aware of what's going on each day.

We do not use hypnosis during our sessions like many people do. I know it was used on me many times during the abuse and programming. Some of the personalities are programmed files, that were created during hypnosis, like Samson and Delilah — the ones who manifested the morning after the first flashbacks and were programmed to commit suicide.

I don't like talking about integration, a term that psychologists use to describe the fusing together of two or more personalities. I don't believe that my integration will be as simple as imagining two personalities agreeing to come together (as it had been explained to me). They were not formed by mere imagination, and I can't see that as a plausible way to be healed. I'm also concerned about the sheer number of personalities I've discovered. Many were programmed or created by outside sources — the "they" people — for particular purposes, such as experiments or occult (demonic) activities. Still others had been born because of the many years of abuse and trauma. I think that if I am to be healed, it will have to be an act of God because I am so broken.

I'm able to function in daily life as long as I avoid all stress, but that isn't always possible. I never know when I might become stressed and a traumatized personality might slip out. Once the movement and shift in my mind begins, it seems as though the line forms internally for the personalities wanting to be released from the suspended trauma that holds them captive. They've waited a long time to release their fears and the pain of their life's existence.

I've started working at a catering company. I really like it, but we work really long hours, sometimes sixteen hours a day, several days in a row. This doesn't leave much time to relax or sleep. I've been working a lot of hours, but my friend Darla has come over to visit today since I have the day off. We are walking to the store to get a Coke. We are talking about nothing in particular when, all of a sudden, a little girl pops out from behind the veil in my mind. She is crying and is severely traumatized, which means that I am crying and acting traumatized in front of of Darla.

She asks Darla, "What are they doing to me? Can I come out?"

I feel an enormous amount of terror coming from her. I sense that her whole life's existence was continuous torture. She has never seen the light of day. She is squinting her eyes. My eyesight changes, as if I've never seen the sun so bright. It's blurry. I can barely see because of the sunlight. *Is this the little girl I wrote the poem about the night of the flashbacks?* I think this is the unwanted little girl who lived in the well. She's never been out of the darkness...before today.

Darla looks at her (me) and asks "Who are you?"

And then she's gone. As quickly as she appeared, she vanishes back into the depths of my mind. I look at Darla and ask her what happened. Although the little girl appeared only for a minute or two, Darla is able to describe what she saw.

"Your face looked like a child, but old and haggard. She looked old, like she'd been tortured." Darla went on, shaking her head at what she'd seen, and adding, "That was weird. You looked so different, like your body was little, but it wasn't."

I'm not sure why, but we start laughing, sort of hysterically. I guess we are both in shock by what just happened. Even though we are freaked out we continue on to the store as if nothing has happened.

As we walk, I feel strange, nervous and shaky. I start going over what just happened in my head. I think I know some things about the little girl. She was kept in total darkness for extremely long periods of time and tortured, although I don't know any details, yet. I think she is about 4 years old. She is extremely fragile: sadness, loneliness and terror are the only emotions she's ever felt. *And now I have to feel them, too.*

I've learned that when one of the deeper, more traumatized personalities comes out or reveals her secrets, it sends a shock wave throughout my psyche and sometimes causes another traumatized personality to be exposed quickly after. It's like an earthquake that uncovers hidden archeological artifacts, or in my case, a mental earthquake that uncovers more trauma. And so it was in this case.

We arrive at the store. *What's happening? I can't see. What is this?* There are shadows before my eyes, only it's like they are inside my head, not in front of me. Freaked out, I turn and run out of the store in a panic.

Darla comes back outside and asks, "Whats wrong?"

"I'm a twin," I say. "Will you be my twin sister?"

Mentally, in my mind's eye, I see two people and I'm in the back. I can see out of my eyes, but I have to look past the two shadows.

"I have to have a twin; I have to have a sister!" I repeat. I am desperate to get a sister. I can feel the desperation grip my mind.

The words are coming out of my mouth but I have no idea what I am talking about. *Why do I have to have a sister? Isn't the twin the other shadow that I'm seeing? So why am I asking Darla to be my sister?*

I feel ambushed by my mind. *I'm scared.* I don't know how to stop this avalanche. I fear the unidentifiable images that are racing through my mind. Dark rooms and people, but mostly, an overwhelming feeling of madness. *Crazy fear.*

I can hardly bear the crazy feelings being released from my brain. I can not identify what I'm seeing, but a mountain of terrifying fear is being unloaded on my body and mind. I'm going into shock. *Oh no, what's happening to me?* I'm trying to regain my composure, but I'm shaken to my core. I can't form a coherent sentence to tell Darla what's happening. Somehow, she is able to get me back home.

I knew delving deeper into the memories would be difficult, and now my worst fears are coming true: my mind is breaking apart and I am overwhelmed. For several weeks after this episode I'm not able to work or function. I barely speak. I breathe, sleep, eat and go to my appointments with Dr. Dixon.

The newly emerging personalities are by far the most damaged yet. The feelings released when that little girl came to the surface are indescribable. The process of recovery is like peeling back the layers of an onion; only I never know what the next layer will reveal. I feel as though Pandora's Box has been opened, and I can't close it. I'm overwhelmed and under-healed. Little do I know that on top of the mental agony that is going on, I am also uncovering a spiritual battlefield that I have no idea exists. I will soon found out how little control I really have over what is happening to me.

The memories I have recovered are still broken pieces. Just as in the flashbacks, they are still disconnected and confusing bits of life that I cannot put in order, or make sense of. I want to know what happened, but it seems my mind is unable to relay the memories of what I went through in large enough pieces for me to fully grasp or understand what I'm seeing. The fear coming out of the past is paralyzing. I wonder if the trauma was broken up into small pieces when it happened? *Could my mind not keep a full memory together?* The thought frightens me so much that I banish it.

The days of understanding are coming, but first, a battle between heaven and hell will be unleashed.

CHAPTER SIX

It's just after midnight. The clock reads 12:20 am. I'm laying in bed reading. Suddenly, I hear the sound of an alarm ringing, like a warning siren. I know it's only in my head, so I don't panic. I've heard this before when a particularly bad memory comes out. I think something bad is about to happen. Let me get my leg under the blanket so I will feel safe. Before I can even complete the thought, I get swept away into the past...

People are all around. They are chanting and talking. A lot of commotion is going on. I am still in the womb, not yet born. They are dedicating my life to the service and use of Satan. A strange thought crosses my mind: at least the relatives can't touch me.

Then, a figure appears close to me, just above my face. It's like a person, but I don't see a body, only a face. It's not like a normal face. It's all black. This face is old, but not just old...ancient and ashen, like charcoal, with slits for eyes and a mouth, two small holes for a nose. The right eye opens, and it flickers. It's alive, and I am being sucked inside of this being through its eye. I can feel it. No, no, no. It's full of darkness. The darkness is magnetic, all consuming — black, dead but alive, and with a chaotic force — a black tornado of pure evil. It's Satan. He is here, and I am inside his darkness.

It stops as suddenly as it began. I re-emerge, and my leg is still uncovered. The clock reads 12:40 am. The memory lasted twenty minutes. As I come back to the present time and regain my senses; I wonder how this is possible? People can't remember things from before they were born. Can they?

Three years have passed since my mind first unleashed it's contents into my consciousness. The memories have slowed, but fear and confusion have increased. The different personalities keep weaving in and out of my consciousness revealing a myriad of emotions and pieces of their lives. By this time, I'm used to the idea that my childhood was not what I'd thought it had been for the first 29 years of my life, but it's still hard to accept. I just want to be normal, but every time I think I'm about to get somewhere, I realize again that the life I've lived is far from normal. This will not just go away.

I'm still in therapy, going through the memories, but I still can't seem to put the pieces of the puzzle together. I'm confused about the memories I see in which I'm being programmed. In the memories, there are people trying to get me to act, believe, think and talk certain ways. The torture and deprivation of all human connections make me very susceptible to whatever reality they want me to accept.

I don't want to believe that people would actually do this to children. I have a hard time accepting or deciding what is real. Even with my persistence and the desire to be healed, I always seem to wind up back at the beginning, unable to make any forward progress. I can't tell — *or am I denying?* — what is real. The memories are so fragmented and scattered I can't figure out what's going on. If I was kept underground and used for experiments, then the things I thought happened during that time, like attending school, can't be right. Roadblocks and detours keep me from the truth. I go around in mental circles — reality versus what I've always thought, or was told, happened.

I don't know why, but I have begun to fear that the "they" people, who programmed and tortured me, are going to come and take me somewhere. I keep thinking they will put a copy of me in my life, and no one will know that it isn't me. *Maybe, that's what they did when I was young. That's why no one seemed to miss me. When we moved, did they switch me out with someone who looked like me so the family didn't know it wasn't me? They didn't know I wasn't even there?*

I have to talk to Mimms. I need to tell him about me. He has to know everything, even my inner thoughts and fears. I want him to be able to know if, one day, I am not me any more, if they've taken me away. I will be gone, and he won't know it's not me he is living with. He won't even know I am gone.

I tell Mimms about the stuff that's going on in my head. I tell him about my hopes, fears, desires, frustrations, heartbreaks — anything that makes me who I am. I hope he's listening so he will know if someone else ever tries to take my place. I hope he knows enough that he'll see the difference between me and a copy. I don't think he understands what I'm telling him. I'm not sure if I understand it either.

Our apartment lease is up, so we've decided to buy a home. We aren't moving far, but the process still begins to weigh heavy on me. As moving day approaches I begin to panic and feel paralyzed. I remember when I was a child and we moved from one house or city to another, the "they" people would come and put me in the underground compounds for more programming and experiments. The family would move to a new home, and then I would just show up weeks, months or even a year later. Everyone behaved as though I'd never been missing.

Moving day has arrived, and I'm a nervous wreck. The confusion related to the moves we made when I was a child are causing me to freak out. I'm throwing things away. I think I have been given things, like a phone, a rocking chair, and several other things that are meant to keep track of me. I think they have tracking devices in them. I think "they" put them there. I'm aware of my paranoia, but still I wonder if I am right. Since I'm so upset, Mimms decides I don't need to help him pack or move. Instead, he suggests that I call for an appointment with Jean Ann, my psychologist, as a sort of emergency. I quickly agree. I'll do anything to avoid moving.

I'm driving to her office when, suddenly, I feel like someone is holding an ether- (or chloroform-) soaked cloth over my face, causing me to become numb and sleepy. I lean my head out of the car window, so I can breath well enough to keep driving. *Is this a flashback? What's happening?* I'm barely able to keep myself awake long enough to get to my appointment. When I finally get to the office, I have to wait outside until she finishes her current appointment. I'm having a hard time hanging onto reality. I feel like my thoughts are being stolen. If she doesn't hurry, I won't remember why I came. *Why did I come?*

A few minutes pass before she comes out, but now I can't tell her anything. I have no idea why I came. I don't remember what happened on the way here. My mind is completely and utterly blank. I feel defeated. I am humiliated and ashamed that I bothered her with my emergency, one I can't even remember! I drive home. Mimms asks me how I'm feeling, but I don't have the strength to respond. I go inside and lay in bed the rest of the weekend.

One night near the end of October, my friend Darla stays over for a visit. She's helping me paint the bedroom in the new house when we decide to take a break and go to the store for a Coke. It's just past midnight. As we go out the door, I see a hammer laying on the floor and I reach down and pick it up.

"Let's take this just in case we need it," I say. *What do I need a hammer for?* We continue out the door. It's raining so hard we have to run to the car and get in before we get soaked. I put the hammer on the floor on the passenger side of the car.

As I drive to the E-Z Mart, Darla makes a strange noise in the passenger seat, and I turn to look her way. She's staring back at me. She's trembling and crying; I can see she is terrified.

"What's wrong?" I ask.

She can barely speak through her tears, but she manages to say, "I don't know who you are."

"What do you mean?" I ask calmly. "What do you see?"

She is shaking uncontrollably. But she finally manages to say "You look totally different."

Somehow, I begin describing what she is seeing.

"I am taller...bigger, and my hair is different, curlier." *How do I know this? I've seen this before? When? When I was little?*

"I've seen this before," I tell her. "I wrote about it in my journal a couple of years ago. I think this is what I would've looked like if they hadn't experimented on me."

"I don't have any proof, and I don't know how I know. It's just a gut feeling." I add.

This is my true identity — the me that God created, the me I would have been if all the bad stuff had not happened. They altered my appearance.

I continue "If you feel threatened at any time, you can use the hammer." *Is this why I brought the hammer? I must be crazy. She could kill me with it!*

I'm not thinking about the consequences of what I'm saying, but for some reason, I want her to feel safe. We arrive at the store, and under the bright lights my appearance returns to normal. We're both in shock and laughing rather hysterically, but once we enter the store, we gather our drinks and snacks and act as if nothing unusual happened.

On the ride home we talk about what we've just seen. We both admit we haven't any idea what it was, but we think it's some sort of supernatural manifestation. We spend rest of the night musing over the phenomenon, wondering what it could be.

The next morning Mimms leaves for work unaware that anything has happened. Darla rides along when I drive Dana to school and we stop along the way at McDonalds to get something to eat. Just as I pull into the parking lot the bigger me, or other woman, appears again — this time under under the bright lights, with Dana in the back seat. Dana starts to lean forward to ask a question. Darla stops her just in time, so she won't see what's happening. She continues to distract Dana by taking her inside for breakfast while, hopefully, I return to normal. We manage to get her to school without her seeing what's going on. The last thing we need is to have to explain why mommy looks like a different person.

After we drop Dana off, Darla and I go to our old apartment instead of the house. I need to pick up a few things that we haven't moved yet. Once we are inside, this other person continues to appear and disappear for the next several hours.

"You look like you are half yourself and half the other person when you stand in the hallway," Darla says.

"You've got to stand in either the dark hallway or the bedroom light. This is making me really nervous."

Even though this manifestation has occurred a few times, Darla is still pretty disturbed by what's going on. She says she's not sure who she's going to be looking at when she looks at me. She decides to call her father and ask him to pray for us. This surprises me since I've never met her father or heard her talk about him.

"My father has a special connection to God," she explains. "A long time ago he was working construction and was buried alive when a culvert caved in. He was in the mud, in over his head, for a long time before they pulled him out. He'd quit breathing. They revived him, but he's been paralyzed since the accident."

"He has a special relationship with Jesus now," she says.

"I don't go to church," I tell her. "And I don't think anyone has ever prayed for me. But I guess it can't hurt." Then, I remember a reoccurring thought I've been having, *I need to go to church.*

She calls her father and explains, as well as she can, why we need him to pray.

Her father asks, "Do you know what your dealing with?"
That's an odd question. Does he know what it is?

"No, we don't have any idea what's going on," she says.

He prays for us over the phone; then right before he hangs up, he says, "Be careful."

How can we be careful? I don't have any control over what's going on, so how I can I be careful about it? We are in uncharted territory, and I can't stop the supernatural world from invading mine.

I don't feel threatened or scared, but I am nervous about the unknown. I've never heard of anything like this happening before. It has never occurred to me that the suffering I've been going through is not just the memories in my head, but is the reflection of a spiritual war being waged over my soul.

I'd been thinking about going to church. I'd never attended before, so it was an odd thought. I felt like I needed to go, although I didn't have a clue as to why. But, I kept putting it off. I thought the idea would just go away...but maybe not. Maybe I should have listened in the first place.

Weeks have passed, and now I'm hearing voices, not in my head but with my ears. At times the voices sound like my friends, although I know none of my friends are around to talk with me. I know these voices are impostors.

They are not human. Sometimes they use words, other times they make sounds or scream. It sounds like the commotion of a battle raging all around me. I can feel the presence of evil and darkness hovering, fighting and flying all about me.

There are days when I'm still well, and nothing unusual is happening, but even on those days I never really feel like the voices are very far away. I try to keep functioning as well as I can, until....

Thanksgiving Morning 1992

I spent the night at my friend's house last night because she and I worked late. It's Thanksgiving and I'm supposed to meet Mimms for lunch today. But as my day begins, I can feel an ominous battle beginning. I desperately want to be alone. I know I'm not going to be able to meet Mimms, but I can't tell him why. I'm not even sure what I'd tell him. *How do I explain something I don't even understand? I just won't go. I'm sure it will hurt him very much — after all, it is Thanksgiving. But whatever is coming, I need to be by myself.*

I leave my friend's house and drive, looking for some-place to be alone, really alone. I drive down a country road, wondering what is going on, in and around me. The voices that have been hounding me are getting louder. I feel an urgency, but I don't know why. I have the feeling something big is about to happen. I need to hurry; why and what for, I don't know. It's urgent.

I see a secluded spot off the road in an empty field. I turn on the dirt road and park the car. And then I sit, somewhat catatonic, for the next several hours while the voices scream.

I think the demons of hell and the angels of heaven are battling over my soul and spirit. Some of the voices are only in my head; others, it seems, I actually hear with my ears. I feel crazy. I know that this is not normal. But I also feel trapped. There's nowhere I can go that these voices won't follow me. I sit and wait, waiting for the battle to end. I'm like a soldier huddled in a fox hole. I can feel the evil spirits trying to harm me and then being pulled back just as they get near. The sounds of screaming, screeching and gurgling, and wings flapping and crashing are unbearable. The noises are not coming from me; they are coming from invisible sources around me. Insanity comes to mind. *This is what insanity must feel like.*

After a couple of hours, the battle stops. Even though I've survived, I am wounded. Whatever's just happened has completely drained me of any mental strength I felt like I had left. Not only is this not normal, this is crazy. Really crazy. *Maybe the doctor was right to want to put me away. None of this is right and it just keeps getting worse. Maybe I'll never get better. Maybe this will just keep happening until they force me to be put away.*

I drive back to the house where Mimms is waiting for me. I haven't the strength or words to tell him what I've been through. I don't even try. I just ask him to take me home. I begin to spend the nights and days in bed waiting, wondering when the voices will return. *When will this battle end?*

My mental and physical health decline rapidly after that day. By December my psychologist suggests I go to another doctor. Jean Ann says she is not experienced enough to help me through the supernatural conflicts I'm experiencing. She says she believes me when I tell her what's happening; she just doesn't know how to help me. She knows of someone who has more experience with this type of thing, and she asks me to call him. I reluctantly agree. I call Dr. Moore and make an appointment for the next week.

Meanwhile, I spiral further down into a black hole. Days pass and I don't dress; I stay in my pajamas. I barely function. My mental and physical health have become so bad that I'm unable to drive by myself to the appointment with the new doctor, so Darla goes with me. When we get to his office, I know he has prayed before we arrived. I don't know how I know this, or why I would even think such a thing, but I know. And I am aware that a different spiritual atmosphere is here. I can't explain it; I just know it.

After our introductions, I tell him about the memories and flashbacks from childhood and what's been happening recently: the voices, the battles, and the other woman appearing in my place. He is very gracious while he listens, and more important, not a single look of disbelief or doubt shows on his face. He asks a few questions and gives me a scripture from the Bible. He says anytime I feel overwhelmed, I should read it out loud. He writes down Exodus 23:29-30.

"I will not drive them out from before you in one year lest the land before you become

desolate and the beasts of the field too numerous for you. Little by little I will drive them out from before you, until you have increased, and you inherit the land."

He explains the scripture represents asking God for help taking back my mind and battle the spiritual oppressors. I should read it, he says, as often as necessary. He seems so easy and matter of fact. The things I describe do not rattle him. He is calm and his confidence is a comfort. He explains that we are dealing with many things, including the supernatural as well as the traumatic events from my childhood. They are all linked.

"The Nazi scientists, along with the records of the experiments they did, were brought here to the United States, after WWII," he explains. "Since then, the scientists and the information, have been used by people in high places, often with links to the occult."

He goes on to say many more things during our hour-long appointment, but I am no longer listening. My mind has wandered off. *Nazis and the occult?*

But something nags at me in the back of my mind. A question creeps in. I had it during the flashbacks, too. *Did all this happen to me because I'm Jewish? I'm not Jewish. Am I?* This is the second time I banish that thought from my mind.

It's already dark outside when we leave his office. *Even though I don't have any solid answers for what's happening, I'm somewhat encouraged, because at least he believes me.*

As we get in the car, which is parked in a well-lit area, Darla looks at me and says, "It's happening again."

I am in the process of visibly changing, again. This time she reaches out and puts her hand on my face.

"I want to see if I can feel this," she says. Then she moves her hand to my arm and leg.

"Wow," she says, "I can feel your bones changing and moving as you're changing. It's really weird, like you're growing. Does it hurt? Can you feel it?"

"No, I don't feel anything."

"Look at yourself in the mirror," she says.

"No, I don't want to. I'm scared." I don't know why I am scared to look, but I am.

Darla continues trying to talk me into looking at myself while she is watching me change, giving me the play by play of what is happening: "Your cheekbones are higher; your face is changing its shape. Your eyes are really dark brown."

I still refuse to look. After a few minutes, she tells me I've returned to normal.

Although this is becoming a regular occurrence, we are still both in a state of shock about what's going on. It defies any logical explanation that we can come up with.

As we drive home, she calls her father, again, and asks him to pray.

I'm deteriorating even more rapidly than before. I'm unable to complete my thoughts. I've copied the scripture Dr. Moore gave me onto several pieces of paper and posted them throughout the house. I have to do this because by the time I get to the next room to get my Bible, I can't remember what I'm looking for. I read the verses out loud several times a day trying to ward off the attacks.

I still hear the external voices. They aren't talking to me, but I can hear them nonetheless. My hands have begun to shake; my handwriting is barely legible. Everyday tasks have become difficult. I can't remember how to cook. I can barely remember how to write. I feel like my thoughts are being taken from my mind as soon as I form them.

Christmas Eve is here. Dana has gone to stay with her grandparents and father for the holidays and won't be back until Sunday. On Christmas Eve Darla and her boyfriend, Bill, spend the night at our house.

Christmas morning Mimms and Bill are in the living room sitting on the couch, talking and reading the newspaper. Darla and I are going to visit her father today. I'm in the master bathroom putting on makeup and doing my hair.

I'm looking in the mirror when I begin to see my appearance changing. My eyes are focused on the upper left side of my head where I have the hair brush going through my hair. I notice a movement on the side of my face. My eyes start scanning my face to see what's there. My eyes move downward and across the center of my face. Along the way I notice my skin has changed; it's now perfect, somehow. No blemishes or lines. In fact, it seems to glow. My eyes are a beautiful, dark, sable brown, not their normal blue. In fact, this brown even seems different from most. As I continue to move my eyes downward, I see my mouth, then my teeth. They are perfectly straight, white and beautiful.

I step back to study the full picture. The person I am looking at in the mirror is no longer myself.

My brown hair is shorter, curlier, and a much richer, darker brown. My skin looks like porcelain. I touch it. My face is satiny smooth. Then I look further down my body at my legs. Minutes ago, my pants were a normal length; now they are about four inches shorter. My legs are longer. I notice my arms. They are also longer. The sleeves of my shirt are shorter. Even my breasts appear larger under my shirt.

I am speechless. I walk around the bathroom looking directly at myself, not through the reflection of the mirror.

Years ago when I had attended the group sessions for people with multiple personalities, I'd heard someone refer to "binding spirits." The person said that sometimes, when supernatural events would occur, he would bind whatever spirit or demon was attacking him. I remember this phrase as I'm pondering what I'm looking at in front of me. I decide to test this manifestation to see if it is demonic. I have no idea what I am supposed to do, so I say, "I bind you in the name of Jesus." I'd heard some other people talk about doing that in class. I repeat this phrase several times, attempting to bind this thing, to cast it out. Each time I get bolder and louder. Nothing happens. At this point I'm certain it's supernatural, but I still don't know what it is.

After a few minutes I gather the courage to walk into the living room to where Mimms and Bill are sitting. I wonder if they'll be able to see it too. Walking through the bedroom, I keep my eyes trained on my pant legs, watching to see if they remain short. Until today, no one else has seen this supernatural phenomenon, except for Darla. I have always refused to look.

Previously, when we had told anyone about this, other than the doctors, they thought we were out of our minds. As I walk in the living room, they both look up at me. Bill nearly jumps off the couch, and his glasses fall off his face.

Mimms stares, and then smiles and says, "Nice to meet you, finally." He sticks out his hand to shake mine. I just stare at him.

"Do you guys see anything different?" I ask.

"Yeah, I see it," Mimms says. Bill kind of shakes his head up and down but is too stunned to talk.

"So you see my legs are longer, that I am taller? You see what I see?" I say pointing to this body standing in front of them.

"Yes," they both agree.

Darla has been in the other bathroom until now. She walks in, sees what's going on and immediately says, "Well, hello again! It's about time you showed up when someone else can see you!"

Stunned is the word that comes to mind to describe the atmosphere in the room right now. We, Darla and I, have talked about this phenomenon occurring for the last several months, and both Mimms and Bill have told us we are crazy, or hallucinating. Now they see it with their own eyes. It's no hallucination. People don't see the same hallucinations.

I want to look at myself in the mirror again. Darla, Mimms and I go back to the bathroom where I sit in front of the mirror while we talk about what this is. None of us have any real knowledge to form an accurate opinion. After an hour of hashing over our theories, I return to my normal appearance. Whatever was going on, the show's now over.

Mimms and Bill go outside to work on his car while Darla and I finish getting ready to go to her father's house to have him pray for me. We're ready to leave when both of us feel something change in the atmosphere inside the house. The strangest calm permeates the room. It's not comforting; it's eerie, as if we are in the eye of a hurricane, and the dark clouds are descending on us.

"Do you feel that?" I ask.

She nods. "What is it?"

"I'm not sure, but it feels like something doesn't want us to go to your dad's house. It feels weirdly calm, but not good."

"Yeah, I definitely feel it too," Darla replies. "It doesn't feel right."

"We'd better hurry and leave," I say.

The feeling of the eerie calm leaves when we get in the car. It's replaced with a sense of chaos and turmoil. I don't know how to describe what's going on. The atmosphere feels crowded with an evil presence, like it was on the Thanksgiving-day attack. *This is not an overactive imagination. It seems as if the evil presence wants us to know that it is here.*

Darla starts driving, but as she does, I realize I can't hear her talking. Her lips are moving, but I can't hear her.

I'm not sure what is actually happening, so I scream, "I can't hear you; talk louder!"

She is saying something, and I can tell she is screaming, but I still can't hear her. My hearing goes off and on for the entire trip. I can hear; now I can't. I can hear; now I can't. On and on it goes for the next twenty minutes.

By the time we get to her father's house and go inside, I can hear fine, but my voice is gone.

Silenced — I can't talk. I'm unable to speak a single word. It's not like laryngitis. I literally can not talk; my mouth won't even move. I can't communicate, but Darla doesn't know, nobody does. When she introduces me to her parents, I say nothing. I stand there, limply holding my driver's license in my hand. I brought it inside so I could show her father a picture of me in case I'd changed on the way to his house. I must look silly just standing here holding the plastic picture in my hand.

Her father, sitting in his wheelchair, begins to tell me about Jesus and His salvation. He's still not aware that I can't speak. *What is happening to me?* I begin to cry. It's all I can do as he is pleading with me to accept Jesus' salvation. I want to tell him that I prayed for Jesus to save me when I was a child. But still, my voice will not come out. After about 30 minutes he stops talking. Exasperated, he bows his head and begins to pray. While he is praying my voice comes back. I can open my mouth. I can't say anything, though, while he is praying since I don't want to interrupt him, so I wait for his prayer to end.

While he is praying, it's as though an invisible tube has descended around us and the evil is unable to penetrate it. I raise my head and peek to see if anyone else notices the change in the room. Everyone has their heads bowed, but I'm encouraged. So many thoughts are going through my head. I will be able to talk and tell him what's going on and why I didn't respond when we were introduced. When he finishes praying, I'm going to tell him about the time I asked Jesus to save me.

The prayer ends. Immediately, I know my voice is gone again. Moments ago I was free; now I feel defeated, beyond help, even God's help. As we get up to leave, I manage to get out a simple thank you.

Years later, her father told me that when I walked in his house that day, he had never felt such evil in all his life. He knew I wasn't evil, but the feeling had scared him all the same.

Darla and I get back in the car. She asks me a question, and I turn to respond when I realize that my voice is back again. But it's too late. I have nothing to say.

She drives me to meet Mimms so he can take me home. Once we are in the truck, my appearance begins changing again. The spiritual battle is raging too. I can feel it, just like I did that day in the field. I can't tell Mimms. He would freak out. He sees my physical body changing, but he is oblivious to the spiritual battle going on around us. I'm feeling very agitated and nervous. I don't know what's going to happen now. I'm not hearing voices, nor do I feel suicidal. I can hear and talk, but still, there's something stirring in the atmosphere.

How can I describe evil to someone who's never felt it?

We arrive home and my appearance stops changing, but I have a feeling, a foreboding feeling, that we can't stay here. I can't explain it; all I know is that it's not safe for us to be here. We must leave. Now. And we have to take our cat, (another one) named Kitty.

"Mimms, we have to leave. We can't be here. Something's wrong, and it's not safe. We have to take Kitty, too," I tell him in the calmest voice that I can muster.

"We have to leave? And go where?" He asks, clearly frustrated. "Where are we going to go on Christmas night — with a cat?"

"Yes, we have to leave. We can go to C.K.'s. She's out of town, but she won't mind if we hang out at her house for awhile."

Huffing and puffing, Mimms proceeds to get in the truck, not trying to hide his agitation at this inconvenience.

We put Kitty in the truck with us and drive to our friend's house. It's around seven in the evening when we leave. We show up unannounced, but Elbert, who is housesitting C.K.'s dogs, welcomes us.

We talk and play games as if our day has been uneventful. We don't mention anything about what's been happening. Basically, we spend the evening in denial. Again, how do you explain the supernatural to someone who's never experienced it? "Oh, by the way, demons have been messing with us and my appearance keeps changing." *No, I don't think so.*

About midnight, I feel like it's safe for us to go home. I have no idea where these impressions and warnings are coming from, but I listen to them all the same. I seem to have some sort of intuition telling me when to go, or when to stay. *Maybe this is God?*

It's around one o'clock in the morning when we get home. I don't feel any foreboding about returning. I'm just tired and want to go to bed. Mimms opens the front door and turns on the light. I step inside before he does, and my arms start itching. Looking down, I wonder what's causing them to itch all of a sudden. I see a red rash appearing on my forearms and elbow. They begin to bleed a little from my scratching. I continue on in the house, still worried about my arms.

I notice something scattered everywhere. *What's this?* There's a whitish, powdery-like substance all around the room. It's on the couch and chairs, everything; it's even under our Christmas tree.

"What is this stuff?" I ask to no one in particular.

"I don't know; it looks like powder, but it has clumps in it," Mimms replies.

We walk through the house, each of us going in different rooms, reporting back to the other what we see.

"It's all over our bed and even on the front of our dresser," Mimms says.

Then he adds in a louder voice, "It's even on our clothes inside the drawers."

I go to Dana's room, and I see powder and clumps on her bed, pillow, dresser, and the floor. "It's everywhere," I yell back.

"Who did this?" I ask. "What did this?"

I feel scared about who did this and angry at the intrusion of my space all at the same time. I'm moving faster now, looking through the house for signs of an intruder.

"Did someone break in while we were gone?" I yell as I go from room to room, checking the windows to see if they are locked.

"Who would break in just to do this?" Mimms asks.

"The windows are locked. Could they have taken the glass out?" I ask, desperate for a reasonable explanation.

I'm searching frantically, looking at the shiny, powdery white stuff as I go down the hall to the spare bedroom.

It's here that I stop.

"Oh my gosh, what is *this*?" The door is still closed, like we left it. But on each side, right and left of the door, is a neatly stacked pile of whitish-colored rocks, or clumps, of the stuff.

It looks like someone marked this doorway. The clumps here, unlike the powdery substance in the rest of the house, are neatly stacked, like rocks, an inch high on each side of the door. *Was whatever did this even human?*

My mind is going in forty different directions. I'm trying to find a reasonable explanation for this...this... this...stuff. I open the door to look in the room, which is unused space. We have a few boxes stacked on the floor, but it all still looks the same...until I look at the closet door. The door is open, and on each side of the doorway are even taller, larger stacks of the substance, about one and half inches tall. Several of the rocklike clumps are stacked one upon the other, clearly defining that these doorways are important, or different.

This is the portal. They marked the room where they entered. HUH? What is going on? Do demons even do this kind of stuff?

I turn and run out of the room to go find Mimms and see what he's found. To my utter amazement, I find him sitting at his drafting table, drawing up house plans.

"What are you doing?" I shriek.

"What? What do you want me to do? I don't know what the stuff is," he says, returning his attention to the papers before him. I realize that he is in absolute denial. He can't figure out what's going on, so he's going to ignore it and hope it goes away.

I have to figure this out. *Who or what did this? What is it? Why am I itching? Mimms isn't itching. It doesn't seem to affect him.*

I go to the living room and pick up some of the powder. I can't really tell what it is. Then a thought occurs to me. *I think it might be sulfur.* Sulfur? *Why would someone put sulfur in our house?*

"I'm going to call the police," I tell Mimms. He doesn't answer me.

A few minutes pass and a policeman arrives. I show him into the house and explain as much as I can about what we found when we got home. He walks through the house looking around at the powdery stuff strewn over everything. He nods his head as he walks but doesn't say anything.

Finally, to break the silence, I ask, "Have you ever seen or heard of anything like this?"

"No, Ma'am. It doesn't look like anyone broke in. Does anyone else have keys to your house?" he asks.

"No, just us. We were gone for awhile tonight, and when we got home this is what we found."

"Well, I suggest you call the EPA, the Environmental Protection Agency. They'll be open Monday," he says.

What?! The EPA? Is this guy nuts? What are they going to do? The EPA! This is not some chemical disaster or a nuclear meltdown!

After the policeman leaves, I start cleaning up the mess. I've stopped itching, and oddly enough, it doesn't seem to bother me now. *I think I'll keep a baggy with some of this in it.*

In the back of my mind, I'm vaguely aware of the thoughts I don't want to think. *If something or someone is looking for me, they found me and are letting me know they have found me.* They are making their claim known. Our house has been marked like an animal marks its territory.

Dana returns home from her father's house the next day. I've not finished cleaning up the house by the time she arrives. I purposefully keep her room untouched because I want to see if she sees the powdery substance. I want to know that it's not all in my mind. Even though the policeman confirmed it, part of me wants someone I know to acknowledge it as well.

When I show her the powdery substance in her room, she acknowledges that it is truly there and I'm not crazy. She helps me scoop it up and put it in a baggy. Up until this point, I've tried to keep her shielded from the craziness that has happened over the last few months, but now I need her to be a witness.

After all that's happened, Mimms is firmly planted in denial. It's not that he denies what's happened, he just refuses to talk about what he can't explain or change. He spends the day drawing house plans at his drafting table.

I spend the rest of the day cleaning, but I feel I'm on the edge of a breakdown. It's not the sulfur that's bothering me. Overnight, the demonic attacks returned. They seem more determined than ever to have me. I can feel their presence. I'm scared, paranoid and confused, and I know it. I feel very alone in the battle for my soul and mind.

I convince Mimms that we cannot stay at the house. So the next few days and nights are a blur as we move from one motel to another, trying to stay away from the demons. The battle follows me. No matter where I go, they are there. I can not battle the unseen forces that are invading my life. After three days of trying to outrun them, I finally give up, and we go home.

The attacks, coupled with the process of trying to clean up the unexplained sulfur in my home, drives to me to the edge of sanity. I become too frail to carry out even the smallest tasks. I can't get up to take care of Dana or even clothe myself. I feel the force of a supernatural army weighing down on me. My days and nights are filled with an evil presence that I cannot shake, no matter how much I try.

The voices are back, even louder than before. I can hear them coming out of the heating vents in the floor. I know they aren't real, but that doesn't stop them from harassing me. Mimms finally can't take it anymore and goes back to work. So I am left alone, each day, with the voices.

My life is no longer about living, or even about recovering from the past. I exist only because I am still breathing. My will to fight is gone. I just want to go somewhere, anywhere, to escape this madness. I'm tired of the craziness and the flashbacks. I just want to be left alone — by God, by my friends, even by my own mind.

CHAPTER SEVEN

The white powdery-like substance has all been cleaned up, but the residue of evil remains. As the battle for my soul continues, I slip into a catatonic-like state. I don't speak unless spoken to. I'm aware of the darkness surrounding me, but I'm unable to fight it. I think it would be easier if I'd just go crazy, at least then I wouldn't be aware of the insanity and destruction that is here. As it is, I am aware of how crazy this all is, but I can't process my thoughts or form a defense. I've even quit trying to read the Bible scripture.

The week following Christmas 1992, I merely exist. After finding the powdery substance all over the house, the spiritual attack worsens. I tried to outrun the battle by getting out of the house and staying in a hotel, but the voices had persisted. Exhausted from trying to escape the evil, I went back to the house and all hell finally broke loose.

Now, it's no longer just voices visiting me. I've begun to experience physical attacks. Demons are beating me at night while I try and sleep. They wake me up, beating on my back and shoulders. I can see them. At first, I wake up and see what looks like my friends hitting me, but, as I tell them to stop, their appearance quickly changes. It's then I clearly see the gnarled face of a demon.

The physical attacks have persisted for about two weeks. Now, I'm also waking up each night about 2 am. with, or without the attacks. I don't want to wake Mimms, so I go into the living room and turn on the television. I flip through the channels and stop on the 700 Club on CBN (Christian Broadcasting Network). *Why am I doing this? I never watch TV, much less Christian television.*

This has continued three nights in a row. Tonight they are showing a story about a person engaged in a spiritual battle with demons. *Well, they have my attention now! Wow, so this happens to other people too. I knew I wasn't crazy!* At the end of the program, the guy on the television says that we, in the audience, should pray and ask Jesus to take control of our life. He says that if we ask

Jesus to forgive our sins we will have a new life. He also says Jesus is the answer to all life's problems. *I did that once — didn't go too well. That's when they punished me by burying me in the grave.*

Sitting here in the room, lit only with the light from the TV, I remember back to when I'd once prayed the prayer the man is talking about. I'll never forget the punishment my family gave me afterwards. But tonight, I hear a quiet, little voice, different from all the other ones I've been hearing recently. This one says, "Go ahead and do it anyway." So I do. I pray with the guy on the TV. I ask Jesus to help me, take control of my life, and forgive me.

No lights flashed, no music played, nothing happened. At least that's how it seemed.

I awake the next day feeling better, but not much. For some reason, my mind keeps going back to the show I watched last night. So I search through the channels until I find it again and start watching it. Today they're talking about how I should pray and read the Bible. So, I do. I've never seriously sat down and read it before. The only thing I really know from it is the verse the doctor wrote down for me. It doesn't even occur to me that a few weeks ago I didn't even have the memory to get to a Bible, much less actually read it.

As the week continues, the spiritual attacks become less frequent and intense. I can still feel something like a dark cloud following me around, but the demonic voices and the beatings have both stopped. As I continue reading the Bible, questions and answers drop into my mind about the truth of what I'm reading and who Jesus really is. I realize how much fear I had concerning Jesus. The truth of who He is and what He is like had been twisted, and I'd been warned, and punished, not to have anything to do with the Bible, Jesus, or God. Now, I feel brave, like someone is nudging me, giving me the confidence to continue.

I have an idea. It's one I've never considered before. I wonder if God will heal me. I really haven't ever thought I could be healed. I'm too messed up. But, I think God can heal me if anyone can. I've started asking Him to heal me from all the multiple personalities, the abuse, the emotional and mental damage, everything. I tell Him that I know He is my last hope — my only hope.

God starts answering my request quickly. I actually drive myself to the appointment with Dr. Moore this week. When I arrive at his office, he is shocked by my appearance and demeanor. It has been about a month since my last appointment, but only one week since I asked God to heal me.

"The change is so dramatic," he says he has to ask, "What's happened to you?"

"I don't know," I answer.

Then I add, "I prayed with some people on the television, and I started getting better. The attacks stopped, but I still feel them (the demons) around me sometimes. But I just stop and pray, then go on."

As our session goes on, and we talk about what happened at Christmas and the new discoveries I am making in the Bible, he says he can hardly believe that I am even the same person. He says he is a Christian, too, but he has never seen such a drastic change in someone in such a short period of time.

At home, Mimms and Dana also notice the progress. I can tell Mimms isn't sure whether to trust the new me. He finally admits he thought it might be a religious personality coming out for awhile. After a couple of weeks, he notices I'm not smoking cigarettes anymore. At this time he, too, is a smoker but hadn't even noticed I had quit.

"What happened? When did you quit smoking?" he asked.

"I stopped a couple of Saturdays ago," I said. "I woke up and started to light a cigarette. Then I heard the Lord say, "Don't do that today." So, I said okay, put it back in the pack and that was the last time I smoked."

Mimms doesn't bring up the subject again. I think he's been nervous enough about all this God stuff I've been talking about, and now I'm telling him that God talks to me. But, surprisingly, within a week he also quits smoking.

I continue watching the 700 Club each morning. One day they say people should pray and ask the Lord to lead them to a good church. I am still learning about talking and listening to God, so I think I might as well ask Him about where to go to church.

I pray and tell God, "I really don't like churches, and I really don't trust people, but I feel comfortable with the man on the 700 Club, Ben Kinchlow. I'd like to go to church where he does."

It is a simple prayer, a request really. I don't think about how or if He will answer. I expect God to say something, in a deep voice, like, "Go to a Presbyterian Church or Baptist Church." Instead the name of an actual church keeps coming to me: Shady Grove Church. It's around the corner from our house, and I wonder if I am just trying to find one conveniently located, so I ignore the idea. However, over the next week the name keeps coming to me repeatedly.

Curious to see what it was all about, I call to see what denomination it is and what time their services start. The woman who answers the phone seems nice enough. She says the service is at 10:30 am. and that they are non-denominational. In a huff, I hang up the phone and say out loud to an empty room, "Non-denominational! Well, I'm not going there; they're probably a bunch of witches or something." *Why do I think non-denominational churches are full of witches?* My own thoughts puzzle and shock me sometimes.

That happens on Thursday morning. Today is Saturday. It's about two o'clock, and I'm sitting on the couch reading the mail that came today.

"I want you to tell My church about your life." Gods voice is so loud, I'm not sure if I heard it with my ears or in my head. Shocked, I look up at the ceiling, and say out loud, "You want me to do what?" In my heart I think, *"Don't they already know about the devil?"*

Rather than respond to my words, He responds to the thought in my heart: "No, they don't."

In my minds eye, I see crowds of people, thousands of them, from all over the world, different races and different ages, young and old. I have the impression this vision, this picture, is His church, and I'm supposed to tell them my story. After all I have been through, I feel shock at the thought that God wants me to tell anybody anything. *The things I have to tell are not the sort of things one casually mentions over dessert.*

Sunday morning arrives, and even though I am not thrilled at the idea of attending a non-denominational church, I feel certain we are supposed to go. We arrive dressed in our not-so-Sunday best, promptly at 10:30 am. Dana, Mimms and I sit on the left side of the church at the end of a row. The singing begins; and on, and on, and on it goes. Finally, after about 15 minutes of the same song, I nudge Mimms and ask if he is ready to leave. He answers quickly, but quietly, "Yes, I am very ready."

We're both a little freaked out by the style of music and the fact that they sing the same song over and over. I start to get up, but first I look down on the floor by my chair. There is a huge man laying face down. We can't get out without stepping over him and he's so large we are stuck.

I tell Mimms, "We have to wait until this guy moves. Then we can make our escape."

Meanwhile, Mimms hands me the church bulletin. I look through it, trying to ignore the fact that they are still singing. I flip to the middle page and read: Guest

Speaker Today — Ben Kinchlow of the 700 Club. I stand up quickly, trying to see over everyone's head, looking to see if it's the same guy I've been watching on TV. I can't see over the heads of the people in front of me.

I whisper to Mimms what I've just read, "We should move to the balcony when this guy moves." I look down and the guy who was on the floor a second ago is gone.

We leave our seats and move to the balcony. From here, I can see Ben Kinchlow. *It IS the guy from the 700 club! The same one I told God I would feel comfortable with and would like to go to the church where he preaches.* There's no way we can leave now. I want to stay and see what he has to say. I'm shocked that God answered such a prayer, one I really didn't put much thought into.

I find out later he had a layover at the Dallas airport and came to that church to speak just for that service. God brought him all the way from Virginia to Texas just for me. This whole strange circumstance gives me the confidence and assurance to know that this is truly the place He wants me to be. This is also the beginning of many miracles God does to rescue and restore me.

The moment I came to know the Lord, He became my ever-present helper. He was with me constantly, speaking to me and showing me the truth about what happened to me as a child and the spiritual battle for my soul that had raged for thirty-two years. On the night I prayed to ask Jesus into my heart, I said, "I did that when I was young, and it didn't work, so why do it now." Yet, the Lord prompted me to do it anyway. Weeks later, He told me that as an adult I had to take back the authority in my life, and give my life to Him. Since I had been dedicated to Satan as a baby, he had legal authority until, as an adult, I chose Jesus — that's when everything changed.

As God spoke to me about giving my life to Him, I saw the memory of when I'd been dedicated to Satan while in the womb. No matter what people try to do, God's arm is not shortened to save those who have been mistreated. Satan had been given the authority to rule in my life, and even though for years it may have appeared that the Lord was not going to rescue me from the hands of the enemy, He always knew He would, in His own time and way. The battle between heaven and hell had been going on much longer than I had been aware of, and God had never turned His eyes or heart from His purpose: to bring me into His Kingdom.

I had entered into a new home with my heavenly Father. He began nurturing and caring for me as if I were a newborn infant. In many ways I was, because in my childhood I'd not been valued or nurtured. He was healing me mentally, emotionally and spiritually. He filled me with His love and kindness as if He were watering a withered flower.

The enemy had been the owner of my spirit and soul, preventing me from being healed of trauma. Even though I had remembered and tried to deal with the memories the best way I knew how, the spiritual opposition and programming kept me bound and unable to get free. I was unable to untangle the past because of the interference. God showed me the truth and began healing me. Once the forces of darkness had lost ownership, God untangled the knotted memories, allowing me to see clearly what happened and even how the spiritual battle held me back. He brought forth the old memories again and showed them to me with His light. When this happened, it was so amazingly different than before. Previously, I would be caught in the middle of the memory as if it were happening in the present, here and now, but when the Lord showed it to me, the trauma was removed. Now, the memories that had been released were being healed, the tiny pieces put in place, and joined together without the panic and chaos.

He took out the toxicity; confusion no longer had its hold on me. Peace and order reigned.

Although I didn't know it at the time, some of the most severe and unimaginable memories were still to come, but under the care and protection of my Father, the trauma was removed before He showed them to me. When I realized pieces were still missing, I asked the Lord about them. He simply said, "These are the ones (memories) that I will hold for you." He did not put more on me than I could handle. Considering all the memories I'd had, even as horrific as they were, there were still others the Lord did not allow into my mind at that time. *Knowing what I know, I can't imagine what could be worse that He would want to keep them for me? I've seen evil at its worse. What more could there be?*

Early in January, as I went to bed each night, I'd read the Bible, wondering how the written words could be correct after being translated so many times over the centuries. As the question played in my mind, I heard the Lord say very gently "I watch over My Word, I watch over My Word." *Strange that He said it twice.* He would continue to say this to me whenever I read it until I became comfortable, not doubting what I read. He was melting away the distrust I'd held.

I'd been told the stories of the Bible and that God and Jesus were evil, not to be trusted. The goodness and reality of Jesus had been twisted. Growing up, I was never sure what was truly from the Bible or what they had reversed for evil purposes. They had mingled the truth with lies and deception. The Lord showed me where His Word had been purposefully distorted, reversed and counterfeited during my childhood. God was patient, kind and thorough in revealing His truth to me. He didn't just shove it at me but allowed me to see it for myself and accept it. He let me ponder the truth He brought forth; then He put it in order and made sense out of what had previously been distorted.

He began showing me how He had been with me all along. It had appeared to me throughout my life that evil was always in control and that God wasn't present, nor was He going to rescue me. But that was not the truth. He has shown me over and over how Jesus was with me even though I didn't know Him and, as time went by, how I hadn't remembered His presence, or how very near He had been while I was in the darkness.

At times throughout my youth, I prayed to God or Jesus, or someone, anyone, to come and rescue me. No one did. At least not the way I wanted. I've come to see that God often works quietly, in the dark, to loosen us from our bondage, whatever it may be. Often during those times we loose our faith and hope because He does not rescue as we want Him to. I was praying for the big, white knight who would ride in, punish the evil doers, make a big scene and rescue me. Instead, He worked softly and patiently over the course of thirty-two years to begin my deliverance from darkness.

February 1993

I've been awakened. I raise my head slightly from the pillow, wondering what or who has awakened me from my sleep. God. It's like He is tapping on my shoulder to wake me up.

As I turn my head to look, I hear Him say, "You weren't mad at them (the people involved in the abuse); you were mad at me because you thought I could do something about it, and I didn't."

A flood of tears comes quickly as this truth hits my heart. *I didn't even realize I was mad about it, until now. I was mad at You, not them.*

In an instant He revealed what I didn't know; I was mad at Him — because if anyone in the world could have stopped the evil, He could have, but He didn't. *How could I have been mad at someone I wasn't even sure existed?*

In that moment all my anger and bitterness was being absorbed by Him. They were taken away; peace and acceptance flooded my soul, bringing even more tears.

The question of "Why, God?" melted away. I no longer needed an answer; it's not important.

From that night forward my soul becomes more and more at peace with what happened to me. Somehow, I feel assured that it has been allowed for a purpose, even if I can't see or understand it. God has truly watched over me in spite of how it appeared to my natural eyes.

Years earlier, while in therapy, my psychologist questioned my apparent lack of anger. She thought I was in denial or afraid to let myself feel my anger towards the perpetrators. I didn't feel angry at them because somehow I've always thought that this was a spiritual battle, even though I didn't understand it. I've just always believed that, even though the people were responsible for their involvement, ultimately they were puppets, willing participants, for Satan. In reality, I was angry at Satan and God. But, I was scared of the devil and thought God simply didn't care about me.

March 1993

The days and nights are passing more easily now. Jesus is nurturing and teaching me about who He is and who I was, who I am. He is building a sense of security and confidence within me. I've never had this before, in all my life. He is causing my heart to trust Him. It seems He is supernaturally implanting it within me each day. He leads and I follow, not knowing where He is taking me or what is to become of me. I don't know whether I will be healed or not, but maybe that is what He is doing — healing me. I have no idea what healing looks like.

Today is Thursday, and I'm watching Christian TV again. I take a break from watching the show that's on and go in the kitchen and wash the dishes. I'm looking out the window over the sink when I feel a force hit me. It doesn't hurt, but I fall backwards. Actually, I kind of fly backwards, about 14 feet, to the doorway that leads into the kitchen. The unseen force seems to come through the window. I feel like I've been hit by a bolt of lighting, but without the pain. I land on my knees. I'm stunned, crawling to the couch in the living room, crying, because I can feel something awesome streaming thru my body. I'm laughing and crying all at the same time. *This must be the power of God. The Lord is healing me?*

"Now? You're healing me now?" I ask.

I look at my arms and legs. I expect to see a third arm growing or some sort of physical manifestation. When I realize what I'm looking for, this causes me to laugh even more. I sit on the floor laughing and crying.

I hear the Lord say, "I am healing you."

Then He adds, "It will be a process over time."

How much time? What will it look like? How long will it take? When will I know I am healed? All these thoughts rush through my mind; only one remains: *My prayer is being answered.*

Since the battle between good and evil has been won, all the memories that were merely bits and pieces, flashes of information from the past, begin coming back more fully. The past now reveals itself in understandable ways, in living color and truth. My mind is now ready and able to understand and process what actually took place in my childhood. The revelations in the weeks and years ahead will not always be easy, but the truth can now come forth, unhindered by the unseen spiritual forces that caused so much confusion and torment.

CHAPTER EIGHT

It's autumn of 1993. I still don't realize Jesus literally knows all my deepest thoughts. Today He said: "You thought you were like Humpty Dumpty, broken beyond repair, and that all the King's horsemen and all the King's men couldn't put you back together again." He said, "No, it took the King Himself!"

That had been my secret. I thought that about myself for many, many years but never dared tell anyone. I really thought I was beyond repair, broken into so many pieces that I could never be fixed. I was like Humpty Dumpty. I was wrong. The King Himself has come to heal me.

My healing begins as Jesus watches over me, and He lets the memories be told, one by one. Over the next twenty years, Jesus brings to my mind very detailed memories, and although I'm no longer traumatized by them, I don't always understand what I'm being shown. He moves me forward, sometimes pushing me, sometimes slowing me down, giving me insight and understanding into the life that was mine.

When the memories are first revealed, I often feel as though my mind returns to the age at which the memories occurred. My thoughts and perceptions are childlike. And so it is that I will tell the memories to you in the same way they were recovered: childlike and broken.

The first family, the ones I lived with when I was very young — I feel confused when I think of them. *Who were these people? What were they doing to me? Why did they lock me up?* I feel terror at the thought of them, then an overwhelming sense of sadness as if I've lost something or someone. Do they love me or hate me? Do I love them or hate them? I cannot reconcile the opposing emotions. I think, "The mother really loves me," but then I think, "No, no, she's mean to me."

She cries all the time. I feel responsible. If I am good, maybe she won't cry. If I can just do better and try harder, she won't be mean to me. I think the other people, the grandparents and the relatives, make her be mean to me. They do bad things. They reverse everything. Day is night and night is day; good is evil and evil is good; white is black and black is white. My days are spent sleeping, and at night I am forced awake as though it's morning. Sometimes she is really nice to me and holds me. I feel bad for not liking her sometimes.

We have guests at the house tonight. Their faces seem familiar — I know something bad is going to happen. I'm four years old now, and I can ride my tricycle from room to room. I race from the kitchen to the back porch where they are talking. As I ride out of the kitchen, there is a bump on the floor that separates the two rooms. Each time I cross over it, I put all my energy, anger, and fear into that bump. I am forcing all my energy into the bump until I become the bump — I am the bump.

I have to escape before they have another ceremony. They worship Satan. I have to go to the ceremonies they have at night. I need to lay very still when the people are all around me. I am always quiet...very, very quiet. I want to be good.

Tonight, it is the mother laying down on the table in the middle of the room. She's pregnant. They bring me in while they are chanting. Smoke is filling the room. It is dark, but there's enough light in the room to see. They put a knife in my hand. Someone takes my hand and shows me where to cut the mother; then with their hand on mine, they push the knife into her, cutting along her side until they get the baby out.

They cut the baby out! I don't know if I am screaming out loud or if the noise is only in my head.

"They are killing the baby! They are killing the baby!" I scream. Then they throw it down the well. My mind continues screaming, *"I have to get the baby out of the well!"*

My feelings of terror from that night lay buried in the darkest parts of my mind. Years later, on the night of the first flashbacks when the memory first resurfaced, I was still screaming, trying to save the baby. In my memory, the baby was still in the well. That part of me was frozen in terror, and time had not moved on. I failed, and because I failed the baby had died. I don't remember the feeling of the knife going in, but I remember where I cut her: along her side, just under her stomach.

This knowledge haunted me unconsciously for years. As I grew up, I was terrified of holding babies. I was afraid something bad would happen because of me. Now I see that because I had not been able to save the baby in the well, I was convinced I would bring harm to any baby near me. My guilt was buried, but alive.

I am so fearful of the grandparents. They seem to be the rulers of the house, the makers of the rules. They always confuse me. I never know what will be next. Will they love me or punish me? Is the day reversed, or is it not? I try to figure out the rules.

What will please them? I must do better. I must try harder. How can I stay a step ahead of them? I make clues in my mind to try to remember what's true. I have to remember what's true.

I hope, but they kill my hope. I think there has to be a way out of this. But in the end, I can't keep up. I am numb. I don't know what to do. *But I have something to do.* I have something to tell, but I have no longer know what it is. They win.

There are some people who drive a white car. Today they are taking me somewhere in it. I am too little, so I can barely see out the window from the back seat. We went down a long, dirt road until we came to the end of it. Here I can see an old farm house. There's no paint on it, and the front porch is falling down. I think it looks creepy, but mostly, I think it looks sad, like it has been forgotten. There are rows of trees and briers away from the house, along the edges of the fields. Blackberry vines are growing over the fence. Corn has been growing in the fields, but there isn't any there now. I can see the stalks left from the last harvest. No one has lived here in a long time.

We get out of the car, and they take me in the back door. They push the wall under the handrail of the stairs. It folds back and opens. They push me through the opening into a room under the house...like some sort of hidden room. I think this door is the only way in or out of it. They close the door, and darkness swallows me up. They leave me here — locked in...alone...in the dark.

Time passes. Time, black time. Nothing to mark the days or nights or hours. I have been here a very long time. I'm very lonely and scared. It's dark, darker than dark. There aren't any windows. I wonder if this is what it feels like to be dead.

I try to hide in a corner of the room. There are movements inside the room. I can't see what they are, but I can feel them. Things keep trying to grab at my feet.

I can hear sounds outside. I listen hard. I want to know if I am still alive. I can hear noises...airplanes...like an airport close by. I can hear the planes flying over. I hear the birds singing and crickets chirping.

They haven't come back. Did they forget me? They must have forgotten me.

So much time has passed. I think I can hear it passing because the sounds are different now. The wind has changed. The sounds of the birds and planes are different. They sound different against the wind and air.

The season has changed again. It has changed two times since I have been here. Another season has come and gone. It must be autumn now. I am still here, alone, but not alone. In the dark. Black time.

On the evening before the flashbacks, I wrote a poem about the little girl who lived in that darkness. I called her "the unwanted inside." She'd never felt the warmth of sunlight on her face; she'd never seen the flowers, colors, the grass or the sun. She'd lived her entire life in darkness. She had lived where I could not. When I left the darkness of that room, she remained there for another twenty-eight years.

Several years after I'd first recovered the memory of the farmhouse, the Lord revealed to me what happened in that room. Apparently, it had been used for satanic rituals, although I do not remember any taking place during the time I was there. The room was filled with demons (apparently invited in by the people who'd worshipped there). The demons had often tormented me, pulling at my feet, trying to drag me out of the corner of the room where I stayed.

Now, I remember laying there, lonely, forgotten, scared, and sobbing, my tears dropping onto a soft fleece-like fabric that absorbed all their wetness. It seemed that no matter how much I cried, the fleece never became wet. I didn't know what had collected all my tears or where the fleece had come from. It was Jesus. He had been with me in that dark room. His robe was the fleece I'd felt. He was with me, the unwanted little girl, in the darkness, collecting all my tears as my head lay in His lap. Jesus held me, and His light shown out around me as far as my feet. As the demons tried to pull at my feet, they couldn't come any closer because of His light.

CHAPTER NINE

I live with another family now, and I have an older sister. They said I get to start kindergarten soon. I thought I was already in kindergarten; I used to go to a school. But this family said I have not been old enough until now? They don't have the changing rules or use opposites here like we did in the old house with the old family, so I go along with what they tell me. They call me Susan, the other family called me Melanie. I'm confused. I don't want to get in trouble, so I don't say anything.

It's winter now, the second semester of kindergarten after the winter holidays, when I start school. After only a few days, the teacher says she wants me to move to the front of the room because she said I haven't been answering her when she calls my name. She thinks I may have a problem with my hearing. She calls me Susan, like the family does, but my name is Melanie, so I forget to answer her. Finally, she writes a note to my parents, asking them to get my hearing checked because I'm not answering her when she calls my name.

I'm not sure what happened after that, but my ears hurt. The father says that maybe now I will remember to pay attention and answer when I am called on.

We've moved to a farm. I like living here. We have a barn and a pig named Arnold. We named him after the pig on the TV show *Green Acres*. I like to play with the cats and dogs that live here. There are many fields and forests that surround the house. We have several small creeks and rolling hills I like to explore. One of the hills has a family cemetery that was used in the early 1900's by the original owners of the house. Our closest neighbors are about a half mile away.

It's Sunday and our neighbors have invited my sister and me to go to church with them. It's a little Baptist church in a town nearby. The pastor talks a long time about something, but I'm not listening. Then he says something that catches my attention. He asks if anyone needs to be saved. He says Jesus will save you. I wonder who this Jesus is, and if He can save me, because even though I like the farm, I still miss my other family. I'm scared and nervous that I might say something I'm not supposed to, but I want someone to save me and help me find my way home. I slowly make my way to the front of the church where the preacher kneels down to pray with me. I'm sobbing and trying to tell him what I need Jesus to do for me. He doesn't stop to listen to me; he just begins to pray, telling me to repeat after him. I cry all the way through his prayer, just hoping Jesus will come and save me from these people. I didn't get to tell the preacher what I needed Jesus to do, but I hope he'll figure it out.

I'm feeling pretty bold and confident by the time I get home. The mother is in the kitchen, so I tell her that this Jesus I learned about is going to come and save me. She laughs and turns her back to me, going on with whatever it is she's working on.

Hours, days, and weeks pass since I went to church, and nothing has happened. Jesus is a no-show. I feel stupid for believing the preacher.

The people who keep me in the dark places have come to see me. I'm scared. They say nothing at first. Then they take me into the woods and tell me that because I asked for Jesus' help, I am evil and they have to redeem me. They will bury the evil and resurrect the good. They will purge the evil from my soul. They will help me become good. My stomach feels sick. It's going to be bad, really bad.

They have another ceremony. They dig up the grave where one of the twins is buried. They put me in the box they got out of the ground. Now they are putting the lid on. Dirt is falling on the top of the box — the sound of being buried alive. It's dark; the smell is awful, musty and rotten. It's too small. There is something else in here with me. Bugs and spiders are biting me. I can hardly breathe, the air is too thick, and the box is too small. I need to escape, but I'm trapped. I hum a song: only the tune, not the words. I don't know what song it is or the words, but I repeat the tune over and over. All my focus is on the melody, so intently that I become the song...until I disappear.

When the people finally bring me out of the grave they act happy I'm alive. One man, whom I recognize as one of the people who put me in the grave, shows me a news-paper. There in the headlines — an article and a photo about a young girl (me) who had been kidnapped by the

Mafia. It said I'd been kidnapped, taken and buried alive. I'd been missing for three days. Three days in the grave. These people, my rescuers, had found me and brought me out. They rescued me. They saved me.

Purged of the evil, the little girl who emerged that day learned not to ever ask for Jesus' help again.

Today my family takes me to see some people they know. I think something bad is about to happen. My stomach hurts. I feel like I might throw up. There are three people sitting at the table in the dining room. I'm standing behind my mother and father, the ones I've been living with for the last couple of years. Across from them is another woman. I think this other woman might be the first mother, the one I knew when I was very young. I can see the top of her forehead and hair line, but for some reason the rest of her face is fuzzy, distorted. My mind refuses to let me see her face.

They are talking about something when, suddenly, we hear a gunshot. One of them says that the grandfather has been shot. Terrified, I turn and run out the back door, onto the porch, and down the steps. I want to see what's happened. As I go around the corner of the house, I see a head rolling on the ground. My mind starts screaming. It's very dark out, but I'm still able to make out a body laying several feet away. Several people are scurrying about picking up pieces of the brain off the ground. *What are they doing?* My mind goes wild with fear. *They've killed JFK!* They've killed the grandfather.

I feel panicked. I *need to tell someone what I know. I know who shot him, and I have to tell someone! I saw what happened. But who am I going to tell? No one.* I have no one to tell.

Part of my mind remained frozen in time, holding onto the secret that so many others would want to know...I know who killed JFK.

Lee Harvey Oswald, Jack Ruby, John F. Kennedy — these are the names they called each other. I'd often heard them talking and wondered if these were really the famous people I learned about in school.

One day, when I am seven years old, a stranger comes to the house where I live now. She asks me questions, like a test. I think it's an IQ test. I'm doing really well, she says. After awhile, she pretends to know me and tries to convince me I can trust her. She starts asking many questions about my memories. She wants to know my name. I still remember getting in trouble for not answering to the right name in school, so I don't tell her my name is Melanie. I just say Susan. But then I think, and hope, she might be here to help me and take me home. I think she might be the aunt from the other family.

She says I can tell her anything, and she will help me. Then I whisper softly, telling her my real name is Melanie and ask her if she can find my real mother. She smiles real nice and tells me she will try. As she leaves, I feel so excited and hopeful that I will get to go home and see my family again. I think it was all just a mistake and she is going to make things right.

Sometime after she left, I was sent into the darkness again. But this darkness was far beyond anything I'd ever known before.

I've been sent to another place away from the family. This place is darker, much worse than the hidden room under the stairs. There's a movie screen on one side of the room. It's big, life-size. I'm being shown films and pictures: happy days from the life of someone who looks like me, but I'm pretty sure that's not me.

I see a picture. I'm five years old (the fall of 1965?) and I'm posing with a very large pumpkin. A person in the room, whom I cannot see, tells me that I grew it and then some neighborhood kids broke it in the street during Halloween. I look at the girl in the picture. Looks like me, but I don't remember any of this. *I must have been sad. I think I'm supposed to feel sad.*

I'm supposed to remember the movies. No wait! I **am** the movies — the girl on the screen is me. I sit here in the dark, watching the movies and pictures of myself, but not myself. I'm supposed to remember these events they are showing me, but I know I never did any of these things, even though I see myself in the moving frames. *But if that's not me in the movies, then who is it? What's wrong with me? Maybe I have a brain tumor. I saw a TV show once about a person with a brain tumor, and he couldn't remember things either.*

The movies continue for what seems like an eternity, repeating over and over, day and night...they never seem to stop. Suddenly, I hear music. The ice cream man is coming. I can hear the music coming from the loud speaker on his big truck. Yes, I can see it! I cough at the smell of the truck's exhaust. "Can I have ice cream?" I ask the man leaning out the window of the truck.

They show me the film, play the music, let me smell the exhaust fumes and give me a taste of ice cream. My mind is thirsty for relief from the torment. I drink it all in — the "reality" they offer me. I want the movies to be me. I want to be the girl in the pictures. If I believe it, then maybe they will stop, and I can go home.

The people who took me to the dark places came back and took me to what I think are underground facilities. They conducted gruesome and evil experiments and programming. They used inhumane cruelty to control, manipulate and break my will. They demanded unflinching and unconscious obedience. They implanted memories of what happened on the outside world while I had been away, insuring that my life and memory would not have gaps for the months I had been kept in the laboratories and underground facilities.

I learned to ride a bike today. Yes, I see the picture on the screen. There I am, riding a bike down the street. Someone, a girl, is helping me. She's holding the bike up until I get going. Oops. My feet slip off the pedals, and I hit my bottom on the bar of the bike. They hit me with a bar between my legs, reinforcing the "reality" of how I learned to ride a bike. I won't forget. I hurt bad. I give up. I must believe. I want to believe. Now I believe.

I'm in the fourth grade now. We still live on the farm, but I don't think I spend much time here. I'm vaguely aware that something is not right because I've missed out on something I hear the kids at school talking about. They say that some astronauts went to the moon. *I wonder when that happened?* I don't remember ever hearing or seeing anything about it, but I don't ask questions. I just listen and go along, acting like I know what they're talking about.

As an adult, I came to realize that my recollections of historical events was always a few years off, but I never knew why until I recovered the memory of what happened during that time. The moon landings, the assassinations of Dr. King and Bobby Kennedy, and the race riots had all taken place while I was gone. The world had continued without me.

I'm a kid, a normal kid...at least I think I am. I want to be. Sometimes I wake up feeling like I've been in a very long nightmare. My stomach feels sick, not nauseous — more like all my feelings are stuffed into my belly. Sadness, fear, loneliness. I don't know why or when I will awaken like this; I just do sometimes. I don't ever think about it for long; instead, I hurry to get out of bed and go play.

At times, strange thoughts pop into my head that I never verbalize. I wonder if anyone is looking for me? I listen to the voices of the people around me. I'm listening for voices with northern accents, like New York or Massachusetts. *Am I from New York?* I'm vaguely aware that I'm looking for someone that I will recognize or who will recognize me. I want to be found. I want to be rescued. I constantly look at road signs, trying to find my way somewhere. Home? But where is home? I don't really know. I think I'll know it when I see it.

But I never do. Eventually, I no longer know what or whom I'm missing or what I'm looking for. Yet, I still feel this desperate urgency. I no longer know why.

Chapter Ten

They have taken me from my family again. They put me in the dark, but it's different this time. What am I doing here? Where is here? I'm lost. This place consists of tunnels, rooms and laboratories. I'm in a large tunnel that seems to go on and on: a maze of trails that has adjoining rooms. It seems to never end. Square lights are mounted high on the walls. They are flashing red, and a siren is screaming so loudly my eardrums hurt. Did someone try to escape or are they looking for me? What do they do here? Where can I hide? How can I get out?

The Lord has taken charge of my healing. The past is no longer a tragedy being played out in present time. The information and memories are certainly foreign and difficult to believe, but they are not traumatic. The spiritual confusion and darkness no longer have the hold over me they once did.

I have a vision: a picture of a little girl who looks like me — a twin. My twin? She is about nine years old, and the Lord says, "She's with Me now." I act like I don't hear Him. I've known about her since the first flashbacks, but I've decided she isn't real. I deny the memories of her.

This is an area I still don't want to go into, but then I begin to wonder. What could be so bad that I don't want to know about her? If there is a twin, what's happened to her? The Lord tells me I must go further. How? I have never been able to fully accept that she's real. I've tried to find other reasons and excuses for her existence. My imagination? My thoughts, almost unwillingly, move further into the past, urged on by the Holy Spirit.

They continue to take me into underground places. I seemingly just disappear, only to emerge weeks, months, even a year later. The family never seems to miss me; they act as though I've been home the whole time.

At the insistence of the Lord, I come to realize the twin was a real and living person. I've come to believe the "they" people switched us in and out, between our home and the underground places. They used pictures and films from the life one of us lived while the other was being used for experiments. They showed these to me over and over until they became "my" memories — the programmed memories that covered the real horror of the experiments they were actually doing.

The memory of the real nightmare, the experiments, is broken inside my mind: bits and pieces, pictures and thoughts laden with horror — an incomprehensible fear of the evil I witnessed. There are no words in the English language to describe the sheer terror of what took place. I have seen evil, pure unadulterated evil.

I'm in a room. It looks like a hospital room. The walls are a light pastel color, maybe blue or green. I hate pastel colors. There's a lot of equipment in the room. The cabinets have glass doors on them, and I can see they're filled with bottles and boxes. There are a few metal tables; one of them has a large machine over it. They put me on that table and put some sort of coat on me. It's white with buckles and straps that wrap around my whole body. It keeps me from moving my arms or legs. I want to move. I want to get out of it, but I don't because now something, someone else, in the room has my attention. The twin. *My twin?* I'm brought face to face with the person I did not want to acknowledge existed.

I can see her across the room. She's looking at me. She has a strange cone-like thing around her neck, which extends up around her head. (It looks like the things they put around a dog's neck after surgery.) I'm still looking at her, trying to decide if she's real. I am wondering what they're doing to her when they inject something into the back of my head with a needle. They've attached wires to my head: the front, sides and back. They turn on the machine. It must be electricity because, suddenly, I feel a surge through my head.

I don't have the words for what they were doing to me, but I find out later they had performed electric shock therapy on me. *For what? What were they doing?* I never did find out what they were doing to the twin.

They must have to choose between us. We are expendable, necessary casualties for the advancement of whatever they are doing. One will live; the other will die. She is chosen to die.

My twin died a tortuous death while they made me watch. Although the images are still clouded, I remember. The guilt I held for years — guilt that I was chosen to live. They used us to compete against each other in the tests and experiments, and I'd won. Or did I? Losing meant death, while winning meant guilt, and more torture. Years later, I decided there are some things worse than death — maybe she was the winner after all.

In the years since, I have come to know some things that as a child I was not aware of. The trickery and deceit they used held no limits. They tormented and cut her apart, all while I was forced to watch. The screaming and crying were more than my young mind could bear. I hid myself as far from reality as I could get. I withdrew into the inner core of my being — a place reserved where verbal communications and exterior stimulations don't compute. I was immune to their torture, or so I thought.

Years later, God revealed to me that she died because of the experiments they performed on her long before they ever "tortured" her in front of me. But at the time, when they played the recorded sounds of her cries and groans, I was sure that her death was my fault and that possibly I could have done something more, or if I had failed in the experiments, I could have prevented her death.

God seemed to always make certain that I felt secure, in His care, and my mental and emotional well being, before He released memories that were still held captive in my soul. My healing would be complete while I was secure in His arms.

CHAPTER ELEVEN

*I never know when I will be taken into the under-
ground installations; I'm just there, stuck in the
nightmare until I awaken, having been returned
to my own bed. Each time, I wake up feeling sick
with a gnawing in my stomach, its source or cause
unknown. Most of these times I just dismiss the
feeling by explaining to myself that I've just had
a nightmare. There will be many nightmares over
the years. Each time I awake from one, I push it
aside, hoping the nightmare is over. But it isn't.*

———————

T he years were 1970 and 1971. I'm not sure why
they chose me or how they were able to do all that
they did. They used cruel and unimaginable methods of

brainwashing to bring my entire being — body, soul and mind — into submission. They wanted to eliminate my mind, will and emotions. After all, robots don't have their own mind, will or emotions. Robots only respond to the commands of their makers: soulless bodies, void of all humanness.

These words are stuck in my mind: the making of the antichrist...many of them.

The scenes that play through my mind have a beginning but no ending, an ending without a beginning. No smooth transitions, no once-upon-a-time beginnings or endings. These were stories of a life untold, waiting to be told, needing to be told. So I will tell it here, and try to describe the indescribable.

The walls are concrete and look like they were once painted a rusty brown color; most of it peeled off long ago. The room is square with chairs that hang from the ceiling by chains. They look like chairs from a dentist's office. The floor slopes towards a round drain hole in the center of the room. My head has been shaved, my clothes taken from me — I'm naked. They strap me into one of the chairs and put headphones over my ears. They blast loud noises through the speakers, day and night: music, beeps, squeals, people and children screaming, news reports, nursery rhymes, television shows, misinformation and disinformation. My mind tries to make sense out of the nonsense. The confusion and loud noises are more than I can bear. Day after day, week after week. Time means nothing. I have no sense of it anyway.

It is all too much. My mind is too full, and my ears hurt. My body doesn't move anymore. I stay slumped in this chair hanging from the ceiling. I've been here a long time. They've come to test me. I must have graduated because I've been taken down from the hanging chair.

I have duties and a place to sleep. My bed is inside of what I think is an old railroad car. The bunks are made of wood and brown canvas; they are stacked three high. My bunk is to the right, the middle bunk, at the end. The boxcar is old, and the rusting metal flakes off easily. As I lie on the stiff canvas, I pick at the rusted walls. When it goes under my fingernails, I feel pain, but it isn't so bad; at least I feel something. I know I'm still alive because I feel the pain. My hair has grown out a little now, and it feels bouncy. Sometimes I lay here and just run my fingers on top of it.

Down the hall from this room is where the hanging chairs are. Since I graduated, I have a job, and that's where I go to work. I clean the people in the chairs. I use something that looks like a vacuum, but it blows the dirt and food off of them and onto the floor, instead of sucking it up. Once I finish, I use a water hose to rinse all the junk down the hole in the center of the room. This person, or thing, in the chair doesn't move. It's wearing headphones like I did. Somehow, I've gotten something on my head, in what little hair I have. I look for the woman in charge, so I can ask her what to do. I see her standing by a sink in the next room. She's dressed like a nurse.

I go to her, point to my head and ask, "What's the law concerning this (meaning the stuff on my head)?"

She stops what she is doing and looks at me. "It's okay to knock it off," she says. I brush it off and turn to go back to work.

They put me back in the chair. Their work was not complete; I failed. A human instinct was still intact. Robots do not care if they have dirt on them. My brain-washing wasn't complete. They'll have to start over. They'll make sure I don't fail again.

What year is it? How long have I been here? I don't want to know...it's been too long. I can feel it.

I'm in a room. The walls and the floors are smooth concrete. There are no windows, only fluorescent lights mounted on the ceiling. Long metal tables are set side by side, all in a row. On the opposite side of the room is another row of large metal sinks mounted on the wall. Gray — the whole room is gray, concrete and steel. I hate gray.

I'm laying on one of the metal tables. A man dressed like a doctor rolls the table I'm on over to a sink. He puts my head near the sink. He goes to the other end of the table by my feet. Now he is lifting up my left leg. *What's he doing?* He has a long, huge needle. It's thicker and longer, much longer than anything I've ever seen. He's putting it in the back of my leg! The pain tears through my body. He keeps pushing it up the back of my leg, into my calf muscle; it feels like it's coming out behind my knee. The pain is so bad I feel sick.

He walks around the table. He reaches for me and holds my head in his hands. He says I will die if I ever tell anyone...then, my head is in the water; he's holding my head under the water. Up and down. Up and down. Over and over. *Oh, no; I can't breathe! I'll drown! I'll drown!* Am I screaming out loud, or is it just in my head? He tells me again and again that I will die if I ever tell anyone. *I won't tell. I promise I won't tell. I don't want to die.*

I'm in a large place. It's not a room exactly, but definitely still underground. I think it might be a cavern. It's dark, but I can see walls that seem to be made of dirt, earth, rock. A large fire is burning. The smell is awful. I'm standing next to someone. There are other people here, too. They're moving things from one place to another, putting them into the fire.

I look closer, trying to figure out what they're burning. *They're incinerating people?* They're moving naked, dead bodies and putting them into the raging fire. They're putting them into a huge hole where the fire is burning. Who are these people? *Are these the copies that didn't make it? Are these like my twin? Did they fail?*

As I stand frozen in place, I notice some small round bumps on the backs of the people who are moving the bodies: massive amounts of bumps, disc-shaped bumps on the backs of the people who are working. The people are black, like coal miners. They are naked, too. I think the discs are attached to their skin, *or under their skin* — many discs, hundreds maybe. Whatever they are, it seems to be burning them from the inside out, causing their flesh to melt. *They're burning the backs of the workers!* Horror fills my whole being.

My mind is so overwhelmed, so terrified, that everything shuts down. The memory is crushed, broken into a thousand pieces, so my mind doesn't have to identify the reality of what it's seen.

Another room, like an office. It's kind of dark in here. There is a man sitting behind a big desk. He's asking me strange questions. He's holding up big cards, one at a time, and asking me what I think the pictures on the cards are. The cards have black spots and designs on them. They really don't look like anything. I think this is an odd game, but I answer him anyway. He seems to be interested in what I think. He makes me feel important.

I'm 12 years old when they take me underground for some new experiments with a typewriter. I'm in a small, dark room, sitting at a desk with a typewriter before me. There's a man standing in front of me. He's instructing me what to do. He says that I'm supposed to press on the letters on the typewriter with my fingers. But every time I hit certain letters, pain runs through my fingers and up my arms. My fingers hurt, and I'm scared to keep touching the keys. Then I realize the keys are wired to shock me. No, no, I don't want to do it.

He keeps insisting that the keys won't shock me again. He says to press K, T, B, A, M, but each time I do, they keep shocking me. I think he is alternating which keys have the electric current: one time I press a letter, it's safe, then it isn't. He keeps convincing me that it won't hurt me. He's very nice to me, even though what he convinces me to do hurts me. I want him to stay nice. I want to please him, so I keep doing what he says.

I'm back in the laboratory again, but this time I'm in a new room. I haven't been here before. I don't know how I got here or who brought me, but my mind and body are stiff with fear and panic.

The lights are on and it's very bright. I wish it weren't so bright; I don't want to see what I'm seeing. There are human body parts everywhere. They are kept in transparent containers on shelves, along the wall, around the room. Many of them. I see what looks like eyes, hearts, brains. Some are larger, some are smaller. *Body parts?*

Are they growing them? I feel...no, I don't want to feel... anything. My body shudders, I gasp.

I'm not sure if I overhear them, or if I've been told, but I know that all of these body parts are copies. I know these are not the extent of the experiments either. They make copies of whole people here, too. I've seen the copies.

I have to escape from what I see and know; my mind is forced to stay, and record what I can not. But it wants out too; it can't handle what it's seeing. It's too much. My mind refuses to store the information. The feelings and knowledge of this terror are being forced out of my mind and into my body. My body is abandoned; it is left holding the memory: wracked with fear — incredible, immeasurable fear.

The fear remains hidden for forty one years.

CHAPTER TWELVE

The family moves several more times over the years, from one town to another, always over the winter holidays. They do this twice while I'm away in the underground facility. This happens in the fourth and fifth grades, and again in the seventh. Missing school and moving at the start of a new year always confuses me. I wonder what year it is—1969, 70, 71? But I never ask.

I missed all the fifth grade. I went to bed one night at the end of fourth grade and "woke up" a year later, living in a new house, getting ready to start the sixth grade at a new school. Once again, the family acts as if nothing has changed. They don't acknowledge that I've been gone or that they've moved.

At twelve years old, the foreboding feelings I'd come to fear are behind me. The seventh grade has just begun, and I'd attended all of the sixth grade. I have friends, and my life is better that it's ever been. Normal, my life feels normal, and although I wasn't allowed to join, I was allowed to go to a couple of Girl Scout meetings. I even got to go to a birthday party for my friend, Nancy. I tried out for cheerleader. I have my first crush.

I am living life — really living, not like the life I was shown on the movie screen. I have happily moved on, hoping the nightmares are finally over.

Then, six weeks after school starts, my father takes me for a ride in the car. He says he wants to talk to me about something. As he drives along a country road, he asks, "What do you think about moving to Colorado?"

I've never been there, so I ask, "Where in Colorado? What will we do?" More questions: "why, when, what about my friends?"

He says he will get a new job, although he isn't sure what kind, and he isn't exactly sure where we will end up, he will just decide where to stop once we get there. Then he lists the names of three different towns, none of which I've ever heard of or know anything about.

Then he says, "We'll move after Christmas, over the holidays." Adding, "You can write to your friends and give them your new address."

I didn't go home that day. I wasn't ever officially checked out of school; I just never returned. I didn't tell my friends good bye. They never hear from me again. No letters, no addresses.

This place has a few windows, and it looks like a hospital. I've not been here before. I'm sitting next to a nurse. I don't like nurses. She has a razor blade with a long handle on it. She's showing me how to cut my wrist. She says that I should cut along the blue vein in my arm near my wrist, up and down, not crosswise. She says this is how I will kill myself, if I ever talk about what I know. *What do I know? I don't know what I know.* All I know is this is how I should kill myself.

After she cuts me, she wipes away the blood, then stitches up my arm with a needle and thread. I sit calmly and watch her do this. I don't feel pain. In fact, I feel nothing.

They put me back in the strange coat. My arms are wrapped tightly around me, crossing over my body. The hook the buckles on the coat in the back. I can't move. I'm hooked to a big machine again, like the one with the wires that went to my head. Time lapses. Blank. I don't know what they did. *Was I drugged? Maybe I passed out?*

They unhook me from the machine, and take me to another room. They lay me on a table. I am watching. I'm alert and aware of what's going on, but my thoughts are unformed, clouded. I don't understand what they want. They keep asking me questions, but I can't talk. My mind doesn't know how to talk. They're screaming at me. Threats. They're going to break my leg if I don't talk. They're twisting my leg!

My voice finally comes out. I'm screaming in pain. But, I still can't talk. My words are confused. The sounds are not right. They make me repeat the sentences and words they say. Over and over. The same words. I have to repeat them again, and again, until I can say them right.

Once I'm able to talk, they ask me questions. Lots of questions, strange questions. What's my name? Where do I live? They ask my me where I go to school, and who my relatives are. I try to answer. I'm not always sure of the correct answer. *Is this an opposites game? What answer do they want?* They keep hurting me until I give them an answer. I make up answers so they won't hurt me.

They show me a small round silver thing. It's flat. They say it is a tracking device. They put one in the back of my head while I was asleep. They tell me that because of this thing, they will always know where I am. I will not be able to get away. I belong to them.

Razor blade, cut myself. Bridge, jump off a bridge. Suicide, self-destruct. Never talk. Never tell. Never remember, or I must die. They know where I am, always. There is something I have to do in the future. Return. I must return. I must come back. My mind is jumbled. Information. Instructions. Threats. Fear.

I was programmed to self-destruct rather than remember the past, or at least the real one. They were covering the truth of what they had spent years doing to me. They took the necessary steps to erase their secrets from my mind. Electric shocks were sent through my mind, leaving me unable to speak, reason or remember. They tested, threatened and reprogrammed my mind to serve their purposes. Their deception, and my truth, lay buried beneath the years of torture. Behind a brick wall was a maze of personalities, misinformation and disinformation, all built to hide their identity and disguise the truth of what they hope to learn through their experiments. They were the builders of the wall that would eventually crumble, leaving my mind looking for the truth.

It's almost Christmas when I awake in a mobile home several months later. We're still in the same state, but we've moved since I had that talk with my dad. They sold our house and started renting this mobile home. *Have I been gone since September?* My heart feels broken, but my stomach feels sick. *I know this feeling. They must've taken me back to the dark places.*

They have a tree decorated with blue balls and blue lights. It's never looked like this before. In fact, nothing here looks right — not the furniture, my bed, nothing. I'm confused, lost and alone. We leave for Colorado the next week. We drive away in our truck with the camper attached, into an uncertain future, pulling the car behind us. In my young mind, fear and optimism battle. *Is this a new beginning or the end?*

We arrive in Colorado the first of January 1973. We drive over the Continental Divide into one of the towns my father mentioned months earlier. I wonder if we'll be staying here, but he says he isn't ready to stop yet. We continue driving west another three hours through more mountains. It's getting dark as we get arrive in the next town. We pull into a gas station. My father speaks to the owner and asks if we can park here for the night. The man is very kind and says that we can park, plus use all his facilities.

The next day my parents tell my sister and I that they have decided to choose this town as our new home. We are here to stay. One month after we arrive, I turn thirteen years old.

I'm at a new school now with new friends. There are times that I look around at these new classmates and can't help but wonder if their lives have been like mine. I'm not consciously aware of what I'm asking myself, but I have vague, flashing thoughts about the children who live here: *Have they been used for experiments, too? Is this where they send the children so they can watch us? Do they listen to what we say?* I'm convinced they are still watching me...and waiting, even though I have no idea why I have such thoughts, or who "they" are.

As I grow and time separates me from the past, I don't think back to my old life often. But when I do, I'm filled with sadness. I still feel as if I need, or want, to remember something, or someone. I struggle with lonely feelings and strange emotions I don't understand. I take a lot of walks alone, looking at the sky, the creeks and trees. I wonder how, in the middle of these beautiful mountains, I can feel so restless. I love living in the mountains, and my new school, but I still feel like I'm waiting for something dreadful to happen. Some days I'm glad to be away from the past; other times I struggle even though I'm free.

I've never been free this long before. Usually it's only a matter of months before someone comes to interrogate me or take me underground. But for some reason, it's taking longer for them to get to me here. *Why are they letting me stay here so long? They've never let me stay in one place like this. Are they finally finished? Did they get what they wanted?*

I don't know how to fit in at school. I try to adjust by watching my friends — mimicking their words, behaviors, even their personalities. I go along with the crowd, silently, unnoticed, like a lost child.

My friends invite me to their houses, parties, and the ski slopes. My father watches me closely and doesn't allow me to go many places, and absolutely no skiing. I go to school and come straight home. He has forbidden me to involve myself in after-school activities.

As ninth grade arrives, I become rebellious. I exert all my energies into becoming me, whoever that is. I want to be free from fear and all my fathers rules. So I disobey. I begin hanging out with my friends. I go skiing. *What can they do to me?* I am in full rebel mode. *Is this rebelling, or am I just learning to live?*

I'm becoming independent, braver. My father is preoccupied with his new business, so he doesn't know what I'm up to. One night I tell him I want to be a cheerleader.

"The tryouts are soon," I tell him.

He tells me, "No, you can't try out."

I know I need this accomplishment. I want to do something, just for me. I decide this is it! I secretly try out and make the squad.

When my father finds out, he refuses to help pay for any of my uniforms or cheerleading camp. My mother doesn't help either. I miss camp, but I manage to make enough money to buy fabric for the required uniforms. With the help of my friends and the sewing skills of their mothers, I make my uniforms. I'm feeling special. I've accomplished something. Momentum. I'm finally learning what it's like to be alive, and free. And with the help of my rebellious attitude, I'm gaining confidence.

I'm fifteen now, a sophomore in high school. I have friends and a boyfriend, and I'm on the cheerleading squad. Life is good. I'm feeling loved and valued. I haven't been back to the dark places since we moved here, but I sometimes still have the feeling that something is wrong, like my mind is preoccupied with a problem it can't figure out. But I let my life's activities chase away any feelings of doom that occasionally creep in.

"Melanie. Hey, Melanie!" I hear someone calling my name. I look around the Tastee Freeze parking lot. I see the guy who called out, but I don't recognize him. After a few seconds, I return to the car and say to my boyfriend, Matt, "I wonder how that guy knows my name."

"Because your name is on your sweater," he answers with a laugh.

Looking down at my cheerleading uniform, I see the name written on my sweater. **Susan**. *Susan? My name is Susan? Why do I think my name is Melanie?*

Although I had been trained to forget, it hadn't taken long for the old memories to begin to slip back through. Only three years into my freedom, and I still remembered being Melanie. My mind was already leaking information from the past. The past that I was not supposed to remember, talk about or ever reveal.

Later in my sophomore year, as I arrive home from a date one night, Matt by my side, my mother meets us at the front door. She says that she and my father are getting a divorce. We are moving back to the Midwest, where we used to live, and I have to go with her. My heart crumbles. The thought of going "back there" crushes me.

How do I explain what happened that night? My soul had been nearly destroyed by the "they" people, and after three short years of freedom, I was rebuilding what was left of me. I was becoming a living soul. I'd had hope. My heart went someplace that night, and never came back. Subconsciously, I realized that I still wasn't free. At any moment, everything I had become could be taken away. *Was this part of their plan — to destroy my hope?*

Later when I learn my father is staying in Colorado, I plead with him to let me stay, too.

"I have my cheerleading, my friends, a boyfriend; please don't make me go." I continue begging.

But still, he refuses to let me stay. I have to go back east with my mother. I lose hope, all hope.

I'm not consciously aware of it, but the source of my turmoil is not my parents divorce. I'm terrified of being taken back "there." *Will the nightmares start again? Will I go back to the dark?* Unconsciously, I begin building a shell around my heart. I don't want to get hurt or hurt anyone if anything happens to me. I begin to shut everyone out, including my boyfriend and friends.

We leave on Monday morning to drive across the country. Two days later we arrive at our destination. By the end of the week my mother has enrolled me in the high school where she graduated years before. I attend classes, eat and sleep. Each day is a blur. My heart is broken. I had gained so much freedom in a few short years; now it seems I'm lost, again.

My parents reconcile and we move back to Colorado. Once we return, I have no idea how long I've been gone. *Weeks, months?* I'm confused. *I've lost track of time?* My soul is in a state of hopelessness and confusion. Being back east unleashed the "Genie from the bottle," and something begins nagging at my mind. *Did they take me to the dark places again?* I keep thinking there is something I need to remember. I have something to tell. Something to do. But what?

Although in reality, I find out we were only gone a month, the damage is done. I can not account for all the time I was gone, but I know I feel wild, like a hurricane is forming in my soul. My mind begins searching for answers to unformed questions. When my parents aren't home, I look through drawers and file cabinets, looking and searching. For what? *Papers, a birth certificate?* I don't know exactly what it is, but there's something I have to find, I need to know.

Emotionally, I withdraw. Darkness is stirring in my soul. I cannot explain why, but I break up with my boyfriend. I lost my place on the cheer squad when we moved. I only go to school because my friends are there. I skip classes and make near-flunking grades. I'm on a self-destructive path. I no longer care about anything.

At home I have as little contact with my parents as possible. At the beginning of my senior year, they get divorced. My mother moves us into a small apartment and within a couple of months I feel like an intruder in her new life.

I spend Thanksgiving Day going house to house, visiting my friends as they eat with their families. They have no idea I'm home alone for the holiday. Christmas Day, I do the same. My mother has gone back east to visit her family.

In January, I begin to make plans to move out and get away. I decide to leave school in the middle of my senior year. I want to begin a life of my own. I try to graduate early, but I don't have enough class credits, so I take the GED test and surprise myself when I pass it.

When I tell my mother that I am moving, she appears unfazed, uninterested, but ready to help me pack. I meet my father at the Country Kitchen restaurant on Sunday evening. I tell him that I've quit school, but that I've passed my GED test. I'm moving away.

He asks, "Are you sure this is what you want to do?" I tell him that it is.

Then, he says, "Don't forget Switzerland. 1984."

To which I reply, "I bet I beat you there." I hear my reply, but I have no idea why we are talking about

Switzerland; except that I'd always *thought* I wanted to go there. *That must be it.*

The week after my eighteenth birthday I move far away, but not far enough. I take the haunting with me. I didn't know it at the time, but the past was waiting for me. Within a few short years, somewhere deep in the depths of my mind and soul, a word would begin to haunt me: death.

They'd let me go, but not before they programmed me to return to them. *I'd never be free. The date had been set. In 1984 I would return or die...death was waiting.*

EPILOGUE

When I first sat down to write this book, I was unaware of the fear I still felt inside. I discovered, even after many years of healing, I did not want to delve into the past or write about it. Talking about it was one thing, but writing — no. That would be a whole other thing. The memories, like those of the volts of electricity coming through the typewriter keys, still haunted me. God persisted, but I wondered what He was up to. *Why write a book?* I insisted that my education was lacking, that I did not have the skills necessary to write a book. After all, I'd missed a lot of school. My knowledge of the subject of writing, as well as English, was...well, limited to say the least! And frankly, I don't have an affection for typewriters! Ten years, and countless hours later, I'm still learning His answers to my question, "Why write a book?"

In the throws of the first flashbacks, I'd asked, "Did this happen to me because I'm Jewish?" At the time I didn't know why I would think such a thing, nor did I know if I was Jewish. I still don't know if I'm Jewish, nor the reason why I was chosen for the experiments.

In 1997 my husband and I travelled with a group to Israel. As we landed in Tel Aviv, I heard the Holy Spirit say, "Welcome Home!" I thought that was an odd, but sweet thing to say. I replied, "Thank you," and quickly forgot about it. Two and a half years later, on January 1, 2000, we moved to Israel and have continued to live there, off and on, for the last fifteen years. It's interesting to note that this book has been written almost entirely while living in Israel. Only God knows the connection, the importance of the timing and why He had me write it there, and not in the U.S.

While writing, I had to look deeper and deeper into the trauma in order to tell my story. The compassion and empathy I was shown by the Lord during those days enabled me to peel away all my safeguards and reconnect my mind, soul and body. His healing was penetrating layers previously untouched and unknown. He reached inside my soul, pulled out the depths of my brokenness and put me back together again, integrating what was shattered.

Jesus looked inside and faced the trauma with me, and as the words in this book came forth, He poured into me a love for others, that without Him, I would not have. The miraculous love and acceptance I received from Him, I've been able to pour into hurting people I've met throughout the world. And even more miraculous is the compassion, forgiveness, and understanding I feel for the people who did these unspeakable crimes to me. I know they, too, were used by the enemy of God. However, Satan does not get the glory.

Ultimately, through the tragic circumstances and events in my life, God has revealed Himself to me in a way most of humanity will never know. He has given me a life I would not have chosen for myself, but I'm grateful to have had. He has led me on journeys around the world to sit with others who are bound in darkness, spiritually as well as physically. I count it a privilege. His love never fails.

I've referred to the people who did these atrocities as "they." I remember the names of people, organizations, and government entities that may have been responsible for what happened. But, I also know that the misinformation, disinformation, and programming may have fed me these names only to mislead me. Or they may have actually been involved. The truth is often hidden in plain sight. Nevertheless, it does not matter. There is nothing to be gained by naming names. My prayers continue for those who may still be suffering under this system of evil today, regardless of the identity of the earthly puppets who carry it out.

As far as the burning of the bodies is concerned, I believe they were burning the copies, the bodies of those who did not pass their tests. For those who like myself, survived, I believe they assimilated these people, (or copies) into societies throughout the world to see how well they would function. I haven't any recollection of how my mind gathered the information, but the visual memory of what I saw in the room with body parts and copies in it is forever embedded in my soul. Some of the bodies were different ages, different stages of development, but they were copies. At the time this memory returned, I had no knowledge of the word "cloning" or what it meant. In my eleven year old mind, they were simply copies.

To my knowledge, the birth of my twin was never recorded, nor is there a grave to mark her existence. She died at eleven years old, never having been recognized by anyone but God. It would take many years of experiencing the Lord before I could finally acknowledge that she'd been a real living human being. He told me I needed to grieve for my loss, but I wasn't sure how. Sometimes I feel foolish being sad for someone I barely knew, but He has insisted this is part of my healing. Grieving, in general, has been an ongoing process. It has been important, but extremely hard to grieve the loss of my childhood, my core personality, and my life; the real one and the one I had been programmed to believe was mine.

He has shown me there is a purpose in everything that happens. No on is forgotten. When I didn't even now His name, He heard me in the little Baptist church asking Him to save me. He was with me in the grave and gave me the song that I hummed, the song that I sang, the song that I became. I finally recognized it many years later -- "What Child is This?" It remains in my memory as a bittersweet song, a time of sorrow and of comfort.

In 2004, I returned to the farm where this happened. With permission from the owners at the time, my friend Debbie, and I searched wooded areas until at last we found the grave. The small cemetery was just as I remembered it, on the top of a hill under a grove of trees. It was snowing that day -- the snowflakes, like frozen tears, fell down my face.

"There is nothing covered that will not be revealed, and hidden that will not be known."
Matthew 10:26

CPSIA information can be obtained at www.ICGtesting.com
Printed in the USA
LVOW04s2358170615

442873LV00006B/9/P